T0280127

Fashion as Creative Economy

Fashion as Creative Economy

Microenterprises in London, Berlin and Milan

Angela McRobbie,
Daniel Strutt and
Carolina Bandinelli

polity

The right of Angela McRobbie, Daniel Strutt and Carolina Bandinelli to be identified as Authors of this Work has been asserted in accordance with the UK Copyright, Designs and Patents Act 1988.

First published in 2023 by Polity Press

Polity Press
65 Bridge Street
Cambridge CB2 1UR, UK

Polity Press
111 River Street
Hoboken, NJ 07030, USA

ISBN-13: 978-1-5095-5384-6
ISBN-13: 978-1-5095-5385-3(pb)

A catalogue record for this book is available from the British Library.

Library of Congress Control Number: 2022939411

Typeset in 10.5 on 12 pt Sabon
by Fakenham Prepress Solutions, Fakenham, Norfolk NR21 8NL
Printed and bound in Great Britain by CPI Group (UK) Ltd, Croydon

The publisher has used its best endeavours to ensure that the URLs for external websites referred to in this book are correct and active at the time of going to press. However, the publisher has no responsibility for the websites and can make no guarantee that a site will remain live or that the content is or will remain appropriate.

Every effort has been made to trace all copyright holders, but if any have been overlooked the publisher will be pleased to include any necessary credits in any subsequent reprint or edition.

For further information on Polity, visit our website:
politybooks.com

Contents

Acknowledgements

To describe this book as a team effort would be a major understatement, not only because it is co-authored, but because over the course of the research and across the cities of London, Berlin, Milan and Glasgow, we were joined by a lively group of design professionals, artists and cultural policymakers as well as by keen and radical students spanning many subject areas. We also accumulated various experts on the way, including advocates of independent fashion, consultants, environmental campaigners and activists. At the end of the conclusion, we list the designers who took part and whom we interviewed for the study. Here we offer our profound thanks to the others; for the sake of space, we do not include their various titles.

We offer thanks to the two principal investigators, Martin Kretschmer and Philip Schlesinger, for their academic leadership throughout the course of the CREATe research project, of which this study was a part. CREATe (Creativity, Regulation, Enterprise and Technology), formally launched in 2013, is the UK Copyright and Creative Economy Centre at Glasgow University, an interdisciplinary research programme jointly funded by the AHRC (Arts and Humanities Research Council), the EPSRC (Engineering and Physical Sciences Research Council) and ESRC (Economic and Social Research Council). We also thank Chris Breward of the National

Museums Scotland for taking part in the May 2016 event hosted by the Glasgow School of Art.

In London, we thank Orsola de Castro of *Fashion Revolution* for taking part in the event we hosted in 2015 at the Royal Society for the Arts. We also thank Zowie Broach from the Royal College of Art, designer Bethany Williams and Lola Young from the House of Lords for joining us at Goldsmiths, University of London, in June 2020 for our Fashion's Futures event, which marked the end-point of the study. Various colleagues at Goldsmiths participated in and supported this work, including Sarah Kember, Janis Jefferies, Lisa Blackman, Joanna Zylinska, Sian Prime and Nicola Searle. The artist and photographer Pau Delgado Iglesias joined us from Uruguay for the trips to Glasgow and Berlin; she created a wonderful set of images from the events. Tania Phipps-Rufus provided great insight on fashion law in the earlier stages of the work.

In Berlin, we were guided through the fashion system by Oliver MacConnell, Ares Kalandides, Alexandra Manske, Bastian Lange, Timo Pape, Martina Loew, Bettina Springer, Agnes Zelei, Hannah Curran-Troop, Marina Nikitina and Clara Brandenburg. We would also like to thank Elke Ritt from the British Council, Berlin, who provided us with the marvellous space at Alexanderplatz for an afternoon conference.

In Milan, our team included Giannino Malossi, Zoe Romano and Adam Arvidsson. In Paris (Parsons Paris), we were invited to share the findings by Giulia Mensitieri, and she in turn joined us in London at the Royal Society for the Arts. And from the newly created Critical Fashion Studies Seminar, we offer thanks to Jo Entwistle, Agnès Rocamora and Jane Tynan.

Finally, we would like to thank Polity Press, and especially Mary Savigar for her enthusiasm for this project.

Introduction

Fashion studies

The speed at which the fashion system has been moving over the past several years is faster than ever before, but it is doing so, unexpectedly, as a counter-movement. Fashion is no longer running ahead of itself. Instead, it is undergoing an internal revolution, one that extends to every nook and cranny of its operations. We might even go so far as to say that the fashion system is unravelling. Many will see this moment of self-reckoning as welcome and long overdue (Hoskins 2014). What it seems to signal is, indeed, a process that is responding, by necessity, to the loud clamour of voices from outside as well as from inside, insisting that this sector has for too long relied on its own charisma, and that this will no longer suffice. If noisy campaigners, including key figures from inside the fashion system, argue that people have to 'buy less' in order to begin to undo the damage done to the environment by overproduction, and if there is awareness that saying 'buy better' is no solution if it means only the wealthy few can afford high-quality nontoxic items, then we can begin to see the nature of the kinds of arguments that are taking place. We are confronted by a rising tide of high-charged debate. Brexit and the pandemic have also necessitated substantial adjustment and change. Currently

in the UK, government encourages the kind of small-scale
fashion designers who play a key role in this book to rely on
British-produced textiles and to use local supplies of labour
for manufacturing. This corresponds with the 'Made in
Britain' ethic, but it is also no more than flag-flying, glossing
over the actual difficulties and the scaling-down of the global
success of UK designers caused by Brexit. Since late 2020,
when Brexit came into force, there have been endless delays
in deliveries of EU-produced textiles. And there have been
problems in getting finished goods from the UK to buyers
and into boutiques across Europe. In the past, many young
fashion creatives in the UK could rely on a few days of
well-paid freelance work every so often in Paris, but this flow
of labour has also been thwarted by Brexit.[1]

When, towards the end of this book, we sketch out and
anticipate the development of a more regional and local
fashion culture, with a less imperialistic role for London,
we do not make such a claim in order merely to shore up a
retrenchment of this 'Made in Britain' type. We envisage a
new fashion imaginary which would entail the flourishing
of local hubs and centres in a range of towns and cities
in all three of the countries we look at here, and potentially elsewhere. Bearing in mind recent writing on the new
localism and also on economies of care and community,
one of the claims we make is that localization and region-
alization would make for a more equitable fashion system,
with employment possibilities for more people outside the
prohibitively expensive fashion cities (Sandoval and Littler
2019; Brown and Jones 2021; The Care Collective 2020;
Dowling 2020). There are then dramatic changes that both
climate crisis campaigners and labour rights activists have
been calling for, which are accompanied by other changes
generated internally with the rise of e-commerce and what
has become known as fashion-tech. At every level, then, there
has been a kind of enforced institutional self-inspection. It is
as if fashion has been required to open its books.

In this current book, our angle is set more narrowly
on the everyday practices of fashion designers with an
explicitly European focus. The work itself began before the
outcome of the 2016 referendum. Despite that outcome,
our vision continues to have this wider lens; indeed, we

have found ourselves consistently moving beyond our initial frame because, in the course of the study, the radicalization of fashion referred to above has become a constant point of reference. And amidst the double impact of Brexit and the Covid-19 pandemic, a whole new vocabulary has come into being. This does not mean that the big powerful players in fashion do not attempt to continue as before. In many respects, global fast fashion companies, even as they endorse green accountability schemes, will seek out new ways of appealing to younger people with ever cheaper bargain-type outfits. Likewise, it is important to note that we are not proposing that every small-scale independent designer has suddenly become a radical campaigner and activist. Fashion, as we point out in Chapter 1, has been, overall, a more conservative sector of the creative economy than many of its counterparts – for example, the pop music industry. The mainstream culture of fashion has only very recently been questioned, so perhaps it is early days to draw conclusions about how far the winds of change we refer to will blow. In the course of this book, we are steering a course between such momentous shifts; the tectonic plates that held fashion together have shifted and we are forced to adjust, while at the same time adhering to the values of the fields of established fashion scholarship.

For this study of small-scale fashion independents in three cities – London, Berlin and Milan – we find a primary home for research in the field that is most widely referred to as 'creative industry studies'. In this burgeoning area, there is a good deal of work being done across many forms of cultural production: the popular music industry, fine arts, publishing, theatre and the performing arts, film, gaming, TV and broadcasting and the social media industries. Fashion tends to fit in a relatively small corner, and this has been the case since the inception, in the early 2000s, of the UK government programme to expand and promote the creative economy. One reason for this marginal place is because fashion has a much bigger life elsewhere in the world of global fashion and clothing production. With its haute couture history and lineage of great names associated with luxury labels such as Dior, Chanel, Givenchy, Celine, Gucci, Prada and so on, the fashion industry has led to a substantial body of academic research as well as taught courses that specialize in designer history and brand management; more recently, dozens of prestigious MBAs in the fashion industry have sprung up. Vital as much of the scholarship and pedagogy is, our current study does not find a home here, even though we rely, especially in Chapter 5, on a range of up-to-the-moment reports on the global fashion brands usually published in conjunction with the online journal *The Business of Fashion* (http://www. businessoffashion.com). One reason for our distance from the business and management studies approach to fashion is that the corporate focus across the many journals and magazines tends to adopt an uncritical voice in relation to the political economy of the field, and it pays scant attention to labour issues and to the vast workforce employed across the world in fashion and clothing production. There is of course ongoing research on the global factory system, often concentrated in the Global South, where most of the fashion and clothing labour force is employed (Mezzadri 2017). There is a sizeable body of work that tracks the poor and hazardous and even inhumane conditions that prevail. Various studies point to the low wages and the few opportunities to organize for union recognition and to struggle for improvements in the work environment (Bonacich and Appelbaum 2000; Ross 2000). Research on the global factories reminds us that clothing production is indeed an essential service, not unlike food production. During the 2020–22 global pandemic, many fashion factories (for example in Turkey) were quickly switched over to manufacturing high volumes of scrubs and protective items for health and social care workers worldwide. But, more generally, every person on the planet relies on items of clothing, day and night, and from birth to death. And the fashion industry employs a vast workforce stretching from those who work behind the counter in busy shopping streets across the world, to those who pack in the new fulfilment centres located in urban peripheries for companies like ASOS or Amazon, to those employed in the global manufacturing industry in the thousands of factories and subcontracted production plants and units, many of which rely on female migrant labour. We only have to look at the label inside any of our items of clothing to see how widespread the location of these production centres is: from

Vietnam, to Lithuania, from Turkey to Bangladesh to China. We flag this whole terrain as in urgent need of more sustained and dedicated social science research from feminist, class and postcolonial perspectives.

The field of fashion studies itself has also fed into the current work. This is now a prominent interdisciplinary space, which ranges from dress history and visual cultural studies to the sociology of fashion, from cultural geography to social anthropology, and from urban studies to postcolonial fashion studies. The journal *Fashion Theory*, edited by Valerie Steele at the Fashion Institute of Technology in New York, occupies the leading position. Throughout our investigation we drew on many of the now classic volumes that have been pivotal to the standing of fashion in the academy. And we found particular resonance in the new sociology of fashion labour (Rocamora 2011; Entwistle and Slater 2014; Wissinger 2015; Mensitieri 2021), where there is an overlap with our chosen main perspective – i.e., fashion as creative economy. Mensitieri throws a cold, sharp light on the working lives of the precariously employed Parisian workforce, many of whom live in cramped flats, earning just a trickle of income that is barely enough to live on, while being constantly seduced by the glamour of the *grandes maisons*. Our preference for a perspective that, in the first instance, draws on creative industries vocabularies rests on the emphasis in this area on the urban policies that are orchestrated by various layers of government, which, while they discipline and constrain the sorts of practices that exist in so many urban spaces, also provide the kind of wider recognition and legitimation that what goes on in the small ateliers, in the home studios, or in the co-working spaces, is significant and worthy of support. Urban cultural policies are arguably performative in this respect. What they name as a cultural practice is subsequently given legitimacy. This is important for the mostly young women's start-up activities. It means grants can be applied for. We grapple with this double bind of constraint and facilitation through our use of the concept of *milieu of labour*. If this is the open-ended spatial web of policymaking and academic as well as administrative decision-making, which provides a range of services from the pedagogic to the place-related and infrastructural, all of which underscore small-scale fashion practice, it is also a space we, as a team of academic researchers, find ourselves inhabiting. And so we are both inside and outside this space of urban governance. Throughout the course of our research, we often found ourselves called upon to play an advocacy role, giving talks to policy forums with ideas that emanated from the ongoing discussions we were having with the designers. This required self-reflexivity at all times. We were also constantly interrogating our own mixed feelings based, on the one hand, on wanting these small-scale entrepreneurs to succeed, since, after they had joined our project, we found them all to be so amiable and interesting, but, on the other hand questioning whether this compromised our sociological activity. And how do the practitioners respond, in the end, to our argument, and our call for regional, diverse and socially engaged fashion? For sure, we cannot take their agreement for granted.

Fashion as creative economy is also our chosen point of reference because the design headquarters and the image industries underpinning this world of fashion production are most often located in major cities, as are the art and design schools where cohorts of graduates in a now significantly increased range of fashion courses are trained for the industry. This is where the many policies for the expansion of fashion education and the frequent tie-ins with programmes for urban development take shape. Young people bring new ideas and fresh thinking into the wider industry even when, as we know, their creations can nowadays be instantly copied and cheap fast fashion versions put into production in the blink of an eye. Young designers are also widely recognized for the new outlook and willingness to experiment that they bring to the industry, even when they often struggle to make a living and pay rent. The research on which this book is based recognizes the importance of all the adjacent perspectives outlined above, and, where relevant, we draw attention to the power of the big brands that can swoop in to offer sponsorship deals to the microenterprises as a way of stabilizing their precarious economies, albeit in ways that also, of course, are beneficial to the luxury brands themselves. In years to come it will be imperative for critical fashion studies research to be more fully concerned with the political economy of the whole system, and to track the shaky and uneven movements of the major conglomerates especially as they seek to define the parameters of e-retail in the new fashion-tech world, and often relying, as we show in Chapter 5, on vast borrowing from global, and especially Chinese, private equity companies.

New ways of doing fashion

Positioning this study in the field of fashion as creative economy also gives us a licence to extend to fashion some neo-Marxist vocabularies. In 2000, Andrew Ross edited the volume *No Sweat*, which was a considerable intervention into the field of fashion, reporting on labour relations and supply chain issues and bringing a wide-ranging neo-Marxist perspective to bear on the field. However, at the time, this spoke only to a limited readership. More than two decades later, the whole political atmosphere for fashion studies has changed and there is a profound openness to these very issues. By drawing on the creative industry approach, we are therefore able to refer to processes of precarization and to the power of finance capitalism. We draw on David Harvey (2008) to consider how monopoly rent and speculative capital function in the fashion world. We also draw attention to questions of debt, especially in the form of student loans (Ross 2013). Various other concepts make an appearance, from immaterial labour to the degradation of work. The bigger challenge for future scholars is to stretch and amend these to take into account the climate crisis. When luxury companies burn huge piles of unsold prohibitively expensive items, not only can this be seen as an act of violence to the environment, but also it connects with Marx's own analysis of commodity fetishism. The work put into making the £5,000 bag is wholly disguised and made invisible by the halo effect and the layers of meanings that the single bag is made to bear, as if by magic. The bag is then quietly but ritualistically destroyed for fear of losing the aura if it ends up in a sale. This single act, only recently reported on, tells us so much about fashion's political economy. But it is of course exploited labour that is most fundamental to what a new

Marxist sociology of fashion would look like. The reliance on cheap labour in mega-factories, most of which are in the Global South, also exists in urban centres. Sometimes it is the unpaid labour of eager interns; elsewhere it is the clandestine exploitation, even modern slavery, of migrant labourers, as became especially apparent during the pandemic lockdown in the UK (Sullivan 2022). Disclosures about sexual exploitation at work also reflect many of the themes in current feminist scholarship, across lines of class, race and ethnicity. In some cases, when this comes to light following, for example, disclosures from top models, brands that have been favourites with teenage girls suddenly lose value and even have to go into administration.

Not only has the whole fashion system now found itself open to constant scrutiny, but so also have all the previous stable institutions been undermined and forced to examine their own practices. It used to be the case that the mainstream of fashion journalism, no matter how well informed and professional, was expected to adopt a deferential stance to the brands connected with leading designers, or else risk not being granted an invitation and front row position at the seasonal collections, and hence not being well informed. This has been swept away not only by the pandemic and the shift to shows being online, but also by the increasing use of social media for fashion ideas and information and the consequent decline of the fashion print media. Online bloggers and influencers have shown themselves to be more tuned in to social change than their gatekeeping counterparts in the now seemingly old-fashioned magazines (Rocamora 2011, 2017, 2022; Duffy 2016). These young fashion writers, who are not expecting the coveted invitations, are free to cast judgements that would otherwise be stifled. They have shaken up the establishment by this kind of openness; many have also become activists and campaigners, while others have created huge streams of income from the brands under the new remit of influencer marketing (Rocamora 2022). With print magazines no longer being the first port of call for readers, the stabilizing effect that journalists brought to the field of fashion has been swept away. Indeed, we can trace the way in which the bolder voices of fashion bloggers then recursively push the formerly deferential fashion journalists inside the leading newspapers to themselves speak out and engage with topics hitherto unthinkable.

This is the wider context that has transformed how we now think about fashion. In recent reports and case studies presented in research undertaken at the London College of Fashion, many of the participants who, like those in our study, are young designers keen to see their ideas brought to fruition through developing their studio practice, have a whole new vocabulary when they describe work methods (Fostering Sustainable Practices, 2021). Instead of thinking only in terms of growth, they endorse other activities that could complement their practices. Many are interested in fashion and community work, and almost all base their work on 'dead stock'. This chimed with our own account and with the idea that 'fashion can be different' and with the concept of 'social fashion'. All of which rests on an ethos of care for the environment. From our own study, we found micro-companies engaged in developing nontoxic ways of producing textiles, including the use of milk fibres. More widely, there is now remarkable experimentation going on far and wide – not just recycling, but also various soil and nature-based activities, such as the use of pineapples or mushrooms or even dog and horsehair for creating new kinds of textiles. The focus in this book, however, is on working lives and on what is required of small-scale fashion practitioners to keep their livelihoods on a pathway that brings in an income and allows them to carry on. These are not individuals driven by a desire to be a successful entrepreneur; instead, they are fashion professionals. And in these changed times, some words seem to drop by the wayside. There is less attention to customers and to markets. The designers need to sell their work, but they now focus on the relationship with the people who like the work as a whole and who share the value system of the collections. They will nurture this community-clientele with newsletters and updates, and they will also host social events, talks and parties, where items from the collections can be purchased. The ethos of the relationship with the community of people interested in their work corresponds to the green agenda. By making to order, there is less wastage.

The chapters

Chapter 1 of this book provides an extensive overview of the field of creative economy research and proposes that there are four dominant paradigms that give shape and substance to the terrain. We are keen here to introduce ideas from art theory and apply them to the terrain of creative industry studies. The adventurous stance adopted by art theorists, as they wholly revise and even reinvent what we mean by art today, also opens up a wider constituency to the neo-Marxist political economy they bring to bear on the activities that take place in art worlds (Fuller and Weizman 2021). In the course of this chapter we also emphasize the need for the object that is the outcome of the aesthetic work – i.e., the art work itself, or the fashion collection – to occupy a place in the analysis. And this means reinstating the very thing the art theorists have in effect dislodged or dethroned. However, the context here would be to show how items or material objects flow and circulate, and how, for example, a single dress worn by a celebrity or well-known person can provide the kind of boost for an independent designer that will trigger a run of sales and result in a cashflow beyond their wildest dreams. This can prompt the interest of larger brands offering valuable sponsorship deals, such that an almost entirely separate level of economic activity takes off, even if it turns out to be just a short-lived flash in the pan, giving rise to a 'precarity of success'. The chapter as a whole lays the foundations for the remainder of the book, and the focus on the independent microeconomies in the three cities of London, Berlin and Milan.

In Chapter 2, our focus is on London. Drawing on some of the concepts from the art theory work referred to above, we lay out the parameters of what could conceivably be a new political economy of fashion, with London as a global fashion centre. We argue that the devastating impact of neoliberal economic policies in the city has reached into the seminar rooms and classrooms where fashion is taught and that the outcome has resulted in, among other things, a significant generational cleavage. For a cohort now in their late thirties (including all the people we interviewed), who more or less managed to avoid the exponential rise in rent for both home and workspace, it is just about possible to keep going, although even for former prize-winners it is an uphill struggle. They have constantly to come up with strategies that might mean temporarily moving abroad or moving to the country and working remotely. In this chapter, we introduce the concept that emerged throughout the period of our empirical work: namely, the idea of the *milieu of fashion labour*. In London we argue that this space of activity is concentrated in the art and design schools, part of the bigger university system. We discuss how these institutions have come to occupy pivotal positions in the fashion world. But the changes brought about by the processes of neoliberalism, including the fee regime for university tuition, have resulted in the instrumentalization of the figure of the student, especially the art or fashion student. He or she becomes a kind of guarantee of economic value on the futures markets of finance capital. An 'urban glamour zone' can be built on the backs of the students (Sassen 2002). They attract the interest of property developers, who have an eye on the high profit margins from new housing projects adjacent to educational and cultural complexes, with, at the time of writing, small one-bedroom starter flats priced at around £450,000. So what emerges is a set of urban programmes that reproduce and heighten existing social inequality. Students and graduates from average or low-income families cannot afford to live in the adjacent new and gleaming neighbourhoods near to their colleges, nor can they, as young designers or more generic 'creatives', afford studio space. And so, despite talk about commitments to widen inclusion and doing more for disadvantaged sectors of the population, the social net for becoming a successful designer counterintuitively narrows. We make the double case for the decentralization of fashion culture away from London and the South-East, and for the new moral accountability of the universities that have found themselves players in the futures market for private equity and hedge-fund capitalism. Through the course of our interviews, studio visits and events with London-based designers, we draw attention to the agility and versatility they must show in order to maintain their professional work. Their own infrastructures require many personal and private arrangements even when their talent gains international recognition. Overall, the *milieu of labour* needs a major revamp with a much stronger policy agenda to support this stronghold of UK talent, or else it will simply seep away. At the same time, change can be effected if these kinds of issues are integrated into the fashion studies curriculum. Graduate students might feel more committed to staying put in their home cities outside London and putting their energies into creating vibrant fashion cultures away from the metropolis. Faculty have a key role to play here.

In Chapter 3, we trace the activities that give shape and character to the Berlin fashion scene. Here, the *milieu of fashion labour* comprises the field of urban cultural policy, and our argument is that, with a lack of high fashion culture in the city and, indeed, in Germany as a whole, it is the creative economy initiatives that, since the early 2000s, have legitimated independent fashion practices, with art and design universities more in the background. In Berlin, it is local government (Senate) that has understood the value of these activities, albeit for city-branding exercises and for building on Berlin's historic reputation for club culture and other night-time economies.[2] We also argue that Berlin fashion relies on this subcultural history, even though the pandemic interrupted so many of its activities. Most significant for the Berlin fashion scene are the social enterprise agenda and the strategies that nurture more inclusive activities for training and for supporting employment among socially disadvantaged groups, mostly women. This takes a range of forms, and it does not mean that the aesthetic and avant-garde elements are subdued or less important. Instead, there is a knitting together of a range of practices, from a small Berlin couture (and made-to-order) sector, to various start-up practices, many of which foreground an emphasis on sustainability, to the activities of fashion social entrepreneurs who have pioneered models for fair and ethical producer services increasingly based on e-business models. The defining element across this terrain is access to sociable space for atelier activity and for having a shopfront in neighbourhoods busy enough to attract attention. Affordable space is then integral to this *milieu of labour*, in sharp contrast to its London counterpart, and we cite this Berlin formula, not in a rose-tinted way, but as marking a potential for a more dispersed regional local model of 'social fashion'. There is precarity for sure in Berlin, where the *milieu of labour* carries a tension within it, on the one hand with elements of support tailored to fit the city's self-employed sector, while, on the other, it is constantly looking for ways to reduce subsidies and lower the social wage threshold.

In Chapter 4, our attention turns to Milan, where we confront head-on the very different status of fashion in Italy, where it is, and has long been, a major industry from north to south. Despite the importance of fashion over the decades for so many people's livelihoods, it has never had the status and significance given to the car industry of the North. It has never attracted the full attention of the state, reflecting the degraded fate of fashion as viewed from a patriarchal industrial and postindustrial optic. Our research in Milan finds a less cohesive independent fashion culture and instead a set of more disparate practices set in a context of disillusionment with the *grandes maisons* and also high rates of graduate unemployment. The *milieu of fashion labour* was also distinctly absent in the sense of a presiding set of institutions; instead, we pinpoint it as residing in the context of family, including the extended family and community. The reason this can play the role of a *milieu of labour* is because of the long-established artisanal tradition and the expanse of the entire fashion sector, which means that there is an extensive skills base and it is possible, through word of mouth, for would-be independent designers to plug into these existing channels, in some cases, as we show, developing a new family business system this time led by women. This leads us to make the case for a female-led, small-scale fashion culture springing into being that partly reflects the new feminist politics of the 2010s, especially given that the young graduates in question are desperate to find a professional identity in a context where the big brands appear to be opaque, if not nepotistic and patriarchal, in their recruitment practices. Meanwhile, at ground level the idea of developing new skills, for example in leather or in handling and working with silk, and of gaining access to local workshops, is not a complicated affair; as older male artisanal workers retire and step down, there is the potential for more young women to discover these practices. With a few small signs of state-led cultural policy activity being directed to independent fashion, mostly in response to radical campaigns to support a start-up culture, we draw attention to the dire need for more proactive responses at city and regional level. This could also in effect rekindle the now lost ideas of the Third Italy and the regional and district strategies that attracted such attention in the 1980s.[3] In this regard, we trace an ironic line that connected the Third Italy with so-called 'Benetton Britain' ideas of the late 1980s, precursors of the major creative industry initiatives of the following decade (Murray 1989a). British Marxist economists and sociologists saw potential in the district clusters of the Northern Italy area, which had come to be seen as the frontrunners for post-Fordist production on the basis of the high skills and hi-tech centres supported by smaller family firms dotted on the outlying areas, but with rapid transport links, etc. As we show in this chapter, this fashion activity of local entrepreneurship (from gloves and shoes to scarves and jumpers) provided some kind of postindustrial potential for the British left, a model that could be adapted and adjusted to support a higher wage economy with more rewarding work carrying cultural value (which is not so far away from our own conclusions three decades later).

In Chapter 5, attention is directed to the rise of fashion-tech, e-commerce and the daily practices of 'click and collect'. We widen our lens here to focus on the new political economy of fashion as it is rapidly evolving. Here again we point to the power of venture capital and the futures market, which see money (billions of dollars) pour into the high-end platforms that have been set up to deliver luxury fashion to customers worldwide. Of course, the question has been about how they can duplicate the VIP-type service that prevailed in the days of bricks and mortar, which is now rapidly being replaced by a range of experimental forms of retailing (Rocamora 2017). Our aim in this chapter is to present an overview, but with a focus on the consequences for fashion labour across the new sites for fashion e-commerce, extending from the logistical labour of transportation and delivery to the packing labour in fulfilment centres, most of which are in out-of-town locations, to what Tamara Kneese and Michael Palm (2020) label 'listing labour', which refers to the often invisible work of describing items in fine detail (from where zips are located to the kind of buttons used), and then also providing more details about after-care of items, as well as preparing items for careful packaging and posting. This is the wider context for a new *fashion-tech milieu of labour*. The chapter also includes three case studies: with one large-scale company and two online-only fashion start-ups. Overall, this chapter emerges from the kind of everyday observation that shopping for clothes has changed in a seemingly irreversible way. From the days when someone would browse the shoe department at John Lewis (in the UK) for example, and find a range of perhaps 50–60 pairs of suitable winter boots to choose from, to a time when a customer browsing online on the John Lewis website, even with the use of filters that will remove many unwanted styles, is confronted with a choice that extends to more than 500 items, as well as sales stock on top of this, with the promise of delivery to a local outlet in 24–48 hours and with a guarantee of easy returns if the goods do not match expectations. This model, as we know, is duplicated across many platforms, from, for example, Zalando, which was set up by two engineers in Berlin in 2008, to ASOS, with a head office in London and wealthy enough to have been able to purchase Topshop in 2021. Sociologically this transformation is formidable for the consequences it has for the retail workforces, and extraordinary given the honoured place of high street shopping in the cultures of both urban modernity and postmodernity. It will require more sustained attention in years to come.

This final point reflects the emphasis in the concluding Chapter 6. It is as if the sociological moment for fashion studies has arrived. If politically it is now possible to reimagine fashion as a more socially just practice, which also reduces its own harm element to the planet substantially, then academia will be a key place for this set of ideas to take root. In many respects this is already happening, and it is not our intention to claim a lead role here. Overall, we have attempted to develop a formula to reflect what critical fashion studies might entail. And we are indebted to the younger doctoral scholars coming up who are already undertaking innovative work on a wide range of socially relevant topics across the fashion and beauty industries spectrum.

This is the right moment for this kind of work to expand and spread across the global university faculties, including STEM subjects as well, of course, as the arts and humanities. Our aim in this book has been to look closely at existing independent fashion studio practices. From this we have developed a set of ideas that have the potential for being rolled out in much smaller towns and cities, and indeed the countryside, aided by the resources of fashion-tech. And this is already happening, often prompted by dissatisfaction with the status quo, for example with sizeism, sexism and racism and all the other ills of the industry. We make the case for a system where fashion proliferates as a popular aesthetic, and we also attempt to redress its harms and injustices.

1
Critical Fashion Studies: Paradigms for Creative Industries Research

Introduction

In this first chapter, our aim is to develop a critical fashion studies perspective that sits within the frame of a broader cultural theory. We write mostly with reference to the scholarship that has emanated from the UK, aware that this is a limitation. We focus on field redifferentiation[1] and, drawing on Georgina Born (2010), make a case for bringing back into the picture the actual (in this case, fashion) object or artefact. We identify small-scale fashion design enterprises as the products of a range of *milieus of labour*, which we define as loosely interwoven governmental apparatuses. We emphasize the low incomes of graduates and the top-down disavowal of financial hardship that have long been characteristics of fashion culture naturalized on the grounds of this being a 'glamour industry'. We also suggest looking to art theory and examining its post-disciplinary knowledge productions, its speculative philosophizing and its recent focus on the imbrication of art into the circuits of financial capitalism. We begin then with the point that up until the advent of a wave of government interest in the UK's potential for growth in the arts and in culture in the late 1990s, there was a relatively small band of sociologists and cultural studies scholars based in various British universities undertaking empirical investigations into the socioeconomic factors underpinning forms of cultural (and subcultural) production.[2] These scholars remained quite separate from those who had already, over the decades, developed expertise in the broader contours of the political economy of media and communications industries, such as TV, radio and cinema.[3] Most of the embryonic cultural economy work had an institutional focus. The more senior figures in the UK were Stuart Hall and Simon Frith, whose earlier work had informed these undertakings.[4] Frith played a key role in supporting and promoting empirical research in popular music; he was the lead co-author of a pathbreaking cultural history of British art schools (Frith 1981; Frith and Horne 1987). Georgina Born extended the Frith perspective in both anthropology and musicology, and went on to produce two classic institutional ethnographies, one about the IRCAM Pompidou performance centre in Paris, and another, in 2013, a monograph based on the access she was given as an anthropologist to the drama department of the BBC as it was undergoing dramatic transformations towards a more deregulated neoliberal agenda (Born 1995, 2013). The early work of David Hesmondhalgh (1997, 1999) also reflected the influence of Frith as he completed his study of indie musicianship. Hesmondhalgh went on to become a leading researcher across a range of media and cultural industries, arguably renewing and extending the older models from the neo-Marxist political economy of media and communications school led by James Curran, Nicholas Garnham, Graham Murdock and Peter Golding (see, for example, Curran and Hesmondhalgh 2019).

Drawing on Stuart Hall, Angela McRobbie's monograph *British Fashion Design* (1998) sought to bring attention both to the institutional role of fashion pedagogy in the UK art school system, and to the spread of small-scale fashion enterprises that had emerged out of post-punk youth culture and the fashion schools up and down the country from the late 1980s onwards – also in the context of high youth unemployment at the time (see also du Gay and Hall 1997). This was prior to the massification of higher education, and significant numbers of working-class youth were looking to their own ideas about fashion, style and music to find ways of making a living, usually on a self-employed basis. Youth culture had produced its own labour market (McRobbie 1994). Hall's work at the Open University (with his colleague Paul du Gay) focused on cultural economy as 'circuits of culture' (du Gay 1997; du Gay and Hall 1997). For du Gay, this later led to Foucauldian accounts of power as traversing the individual body and shaping 'conduct' in these cultural milieus in more dispersed and variegated ways than the Marxist model of power had permitted.[5] Hall (1988) was concerned with the changes sweeping through political life, especially the rise of enterprise culture, as the British government pursued further rounds of privatization and deregulation during the Thatcher years and beyond. Both writers recognized the potency of the idea that individuals should become 'entrepreneurs of the self'. There was a constant tension in Hall's analysis between and across levels of activities as they took place in everyday life, for example in the perceived pleasures of consumer culture, and their articulation with dominant political discourse. From the mid-1980s onwards, he and his colleagues had also been writing in a more popular journalistic vein for the magazine *Marxism Today*, which in turn was trying to find ways of modernizing and updating the left to account for the changes in the everyday landscapes of the electorate, especially those sectors of the working class that had been won over by the ideas of Thatcherism. As we show in Chapter 4, this was the context in which ideas about the role of the designer and the attractions of lifestyle came to the fore, not to be dismissed as mere capitalist distractions, but as topics for close interrogation regarding both new modes of production (in an era of post-Fordism) and consumption. The latter was significant for what it revealed about the state of class consciousness at a time when various voices from lesbian and gay as well as black and Asian communities were insisting on their own distinctive cultural agendas.

Still, no one on the *Marxism Today* left, or indeed in the sociology departments, might have imagined that there would be a surge of interest in these areas of activity from 1997 onwards with the new prominence of the Department for Culture, Media and Sport (DCMS), and the enthusiasm of the prime minister for Britain's 'talent-led economy'. Nor was there any idea that, under New Labour, there would come into being such a substantial area for investment and expansion of new subject areas in academia.[6] The cultural and creative industries became, in effect, New Labour's version of the former Labour leader Harold Wilson's famous agenda for economic growth based on the 'white heat of technology'. There was some expediency on the part of university deans and heads of department who, early in the 2000s, saw potential for growth and for the creation of new institutes and posts in an area favoured by government, which also promised to build more bridges between the arts and humanities and the postgraduate labour market. New fields of research emerged alongside emerging areas for study and for Master's qualifications, and if such a terrain gained visibility from the year 2000, by 2020 it had become a full-blown field of specialism and expertise, finding equivalences in Europe, the US, Australia, China and Southeast Asia, South America and Africa, as the notion of global creative economy took root (Alacovska and Gill 2019). Of course, this is a contested and contentious set of developments, reiterating a logic of cultural imperialism, this time in the guise of training modules for self-entrepreneurship in the arts and creative sectors as a globally relevant unfolding. However, already by 2010 a good deal of this energy at government level had been expended and then quickly burnt out, and arguably the universities were delegated from then on by Conservative-led governments to carry on with this kind of activity under the rubric of 'employability'. In effect, this meant professional-izing and providing business frameworks for what previously had been either a set of informal self-organized creative activities, or, in the case of fashion, had been inadequately presented as a career pathway, one that was now in need of more clearly defined direction.

A series of paradigms have characterized this field of inquiry.[7] They are (a) the cultural policy paradigm, (b) the *milieu of labour* (space and time), (c) art theory, as it has emerged from art history and political aesthetics, and (d) the aesthetics of the object (Born 2010). There is overlap and hybridity across these and, bearing in mind that fashion is our field of study, in the pages that follow we make a series of assessments about how they each contribute to the analysis. In cultural policy debate, arguably, the specifics of sectoral differences need to be more fully fleshed out. It becomes more pressing and relevant to distinguish between the different areas of activity, given the opportunistic grouping together that has taken place for politically expedient reasons in the context of the changes in higher education. We aim here to disband the creative industries so that they can be examined one sector at a time. The *milieu of labour* comprises enabling and activating practices spearheaded by urban policy initiatives, such as specialist 'flagship' universities recently repositioned to enhance monopoly rent. The activating practices also extend to many neighbourhoods, streets, lanes, cafés, subsidized studios, digital platforms, all designated for 'economic refiguration' (Loew 2013). The precise alignment varies from town to town, from city to city, and from region to region, each bringing into play potentials and limitations. Some activities are curbed, others unleashed. Given the range of spatial locations which this current investigation traverses, Foucault's open-ended and expansive concept of milieu works well for our purposes (Foucault 2004; Berry 2015). In the pages that follow we also propose that sociologists of creative labour need to attend more closely to the writings associated with art theory. And finally, we suggest the importance of focusing on the objects of creative labour: in our case the hats, photographs, catwalks, coats and dresses, etc, since these are, after all, the *raison d'être* of this occupational sector. What would it mean to reinstate the art and design objects themselves? And how might this be done? Can an updated sociology of aesthetics occupy a new place in creative economy research and in critical fashion studies?[8] How might this nowadays differ from simply indicating a return to textual or visual analysis? How can we bring clothes into conversation with the political economy that spawns them?[9] In Chapters 2, 3 and 4 we sketch out how this attention to the material object allows the researcher to gain a better understanding of the day-to-day meaning of the work that is being undertaken and how it fits in with the various classifications and genres in place across the field. This is often missing in existing accounts where creative industry research tends not to stop to look

at the paintings on the wall or the guitar riff being played
or the staging of a performance.

Cultural policy

Three key approaches have dominated cultural policy
discourse in recent years. These are (a) the critique of
the 'Florida effect' and the writing mostly associated with
the *International Journal of Cultural Policy*; (b) Philip
Schlesinger's participatory model; and (c) the 'new inequalities' work (see, among others, Florida 2004; McGuigan
2005; O'Brien 2008; Schlesinger 2013; Oakley and O'Brien
2016; O'Brien et al. 2018). In the early 2000s, Richard
Florida's celebratory bringing together of a so-called 'creative
class' with emerging patterns of urban growth, as well as
his happy-snappy quick-fix solutions, led to city governments and local authorities across the world buying into
this form of instant regeneration based on culture and
creativity, often precisely because the overall costs promised
to be low compared to what would be required to improve
infrastructure, create jobs and tackle poverty, a word that
did not appear in the Florida lexicon. The impact of Jamie
Peck's critique of this 'Florida effect' has been substantial
in academic circles, alongside that of David Harvey and
others who, over the years, have taken aim at 'neoliberal
urbanism' and the entrepreneurial city for the devastation
they have wrought on low-income citizens (Peck 2005;
Harvey 2012).[10] The tide has now turned, with even Florida
himself revising and pulling back from his earlier celebratory
account.[11] Urban planners and city councils are certainly
less enamoured by these ideas. With reduced budgets and
with issues like housing and rent levels under the spotlight,
the creative class is now held to account. One weakness in
Peck's and Harvey's critiques however is that there is little
attempt to understand how Florida had such traction on the
ground. How was this ideological groundwork laid? Instead
their tone is indignant in a kind of 'I told you so' way. But
it is important to be able to interrogate that time of 'third
way' politics (Giddens 1998). The euphoric atmosphere
suggested that creativity might provide a less abrasive version

of neoliberalism, one that was then interwoven with more social democratic elements such as New Labour's dropping of museum charges (see Hesmondhalgh et al. 2018; see also the interviews carried out by Gross 2020).[12] This action highlighted the distinctiveness of the rolling out of neoliberalism as applied to culture and the arts in the UK and under the auspices of New Labour. Creativity also played a leading role in the redefinition of work, a *dispositif* for labour reform by shortcircuiting traditional and unionized employment and instead promising rewarding or self-expressive careers to the media arts graduate population (McRobbie 2016). Who was thinking about relinquishing labour rights and social protection when being dazzled with the idea of becoming part of the talent-led economy? Nowadays we need to recalibrate the link between the more subdued rolling-out of Florida-esque projects and the heightened resistance by urban activists and the impact of these waves of protest. In some instances, we see that policymakers and city councils will take on board elements of the radical interventions, and thus, in the next unfolding of regeneration plans, appear to listen to at least some of these voices.[13] What needs to be investigated then is the legacy of Florida, and whether 'creative city' branding and marketing as substitutes for infrastructural investment have been modified in the light of the anti-Florida voices.[14] Kate Oakley and Jonathan Ward (2018) have usefully summarized the ways in which recent creative economy research has developed so as to fully integrate the many critiques of the gentrification effect, while retaining a focus on the working lives of this stratum of the workforce.

A *participatory* approach to cultural policy is outlined by Philip Schlesinger (2013). This is the model of the cultural policy academic as adviser and expert, something that fitted more comfortably with academic research in times of social democratic government, where it would mean advising on arts policies, or on regional film boards, or being elected to serve as a member of the BBC Trust, etc. Schlesinger notes that this tradition was more or less swept away in the UK with New Labour's excitement about the growth potential of the creative economy. The focus then shifted to a search for 'ideas' emerging from think-tanks. Schlesinger points to the diminishing role for the public service academic, and the replacement of 'democratic engagement' with fast-tracked experts, all brought into a realm characterized by a 'market-driven model of the knowledge class'. His model does not suggest a past golden age, but it does point to a changed landscape. And there is tremendous variation that exists from one sector to the next, from one region or city to the next. Some culture industries, such as fashion, are more conservative than others. A top-down policy focus reliant on co-opting a limited number of parties means there is little space for social science or cultural studies scholars to gain entrance to those spaces where policy decisions are made. This is different from, for example, the working relations that many media studies scholars like Schlesinger have had over the years with the BFI (British Film Council), or with the BBC. Schlesinger's comments about the marginalization of culture and the arts ring true, especially in the context of the current UK government. The DCMS has shrunk in importance, and, in the context of Brexit, organizations such as NESTA (National Endowment for Science, Technology and the Arts) and the Creative Industries Federation perform a front-facing role. Reflecting the influence of economics and 'return on investment' models, many papers and reports published since the mid-2010s are focused on measuring the value of culture and the scale of the sector as a whole.[15]

This shift to measurement coincides with the quantitative *inequality* work led in the UK by David O'Brien, Kate Oakley and Mark Banks and driven by concerns about social exclusion from the arts, and the preponderance of middle-class and white graduates from comfortable backgrounds across many, if not all, sectors of the arts and cultural life (O'Brien 2008; Banks and Oakley 2016; Oakley and O'Brien 2016; O'Brien et al. 2017; O'Brien et al. 2018; O'Brien et al. 2021). This recent pathway for research reflects the rise of big data as an influential shaper of policy discourse along with the requirement for academics to produce evidence-based longitudinal impact-oriented research (see O'Brien et al. 2018). We might also see the direction undertaken by O'Brien and Oakley as marking a strategic move away from the hinterlands of critical cultural policy discourse. This kind of work speaks more directly to government through collaborating with newspapers like the *Guardian* or with the

BBC, where the results have been headlined. The quantitative element produces vivid visualized 'big data' showing, for instance, how working-class and BAME (black, Asian and minority ethnic) people are increasingly marginalized from participation in theatre arts and elsewhere across the cultural world.[16] This proximity to policymakers seems promising, and the commitment on the part of key figures to effecting radical change across a whole range of cultural inequalities is important. But we must bear in mind the scale of the structural changes needed to even begin to redress these inequalities. To take one example, to put back in place just some of the conditions that made it possible for a small number of black and Asian British artists to emerge from the mid-1980s to the mid-1990s (Isaac Julien, Chila Kumari Burman, Sonia Boyce, Chris Ofili, Yinka Shonibare, Steve McQueen) would require not just free higher education, but also access routes from school via youth centres and community groups, as well as well-trained and available professionals whose job it would be to implement various access initiatives. There was a whole ensemble of bureaucratic, social democratic measures (even subsidized social housing for artists in place[17]) which have long since been consigned to history. An additional point arises which is how the neoliberal *dispositifs* have had their effect. These vocabularies are now being used by so many people employed in the cultural fields that they have entered into the routines of working lives and this makes it hard to envisage a reversal or a dramatic shift to a more egalitarian ethos. The terminology of the New Public Management (the ethos introduced across state institutions from the late 1980s, which favoured competition and tendering, privatization and deregulation, and the introduction of aggressive corporate-style management across the public sector) has pervaded arts and cultural administration. These values have been adopted across the many official training and mentoring programmes such that it would take a lot to dislodge them in favour of a more collectivist way of thinking. The new inequalities work in creative industry research may well jump generations and appeal mostly to current students and postgraduates more aware of social justice issues.

For critical fashion studies these questions have salience. While it is a predominantly female sector, black and Asian and other ethnic minority design professionals are still under-represented. It is also a sector defined by the upper-class style of *Vogue* magazine (only very recently challenged by the arrival of the first black person as editor, Edward Enninful). High fashion culture has historically looked to recruit from the upper middle classes. A tokenistic presence of working-class star fashion designers such as Alexander McQueen, often patronized for their backgrounds, remains a recurring phenomenon. A class bias, together with the exclusion of disadvantaged and ethnic minority people, is aggravated by editorial disapproval for bringing to light social issues such as racism and poor pay and work conditions. In fashion circles, topics such as poverty, hardship, unemployment and trade union membership have rarely been discussed. The value, then, of taking a sector-specific stance when considering which policy strategies to take on is that the historically embedded cultures of work and organizational practices can be better understood (Bull 2019; Bull and Scharff 2017). In fashion, this would mean challenging the assumptions underpinning the agenda of leading organizations such as the British Fashion Council, and it would also mean initiating a debate about the curriculum in university fashion departments up and down the country. There needs to be discussion about the prevailing cultural values that inform the professional codes and working practices in fashion, including the rigid hierarchies that accrue from the myth of the creative genius and the *auteur* image of the designer (Mensitieri 2021).

Milieu of labour

Space and labour have shown themselves to be among the most enduring concepts in creative economy research. We signal here their interconnectedness, the way in which they bend into one another. We use the phrase *milieu of labour*, borrowing from Josephine Berry's (2015) use of the term *milieu* in her analysis of regeneration and cultural politics in London's Olympic Park. The value here is that this term suggests a 'flexi' space created and maintained by modes of governmentality which then constantly and recursively insert themselves back into these same spaces, as a form of 'optimization'. Berry shows how those who live in the surrounding neighbourhood of Olympic Park, a largely low-income population in typically poor-quality housing, are invited to enjoy the various curated spectacles, in particular public art that is, in reality, there to enhance the speculative force of financial capital as it has descended on this formerly postindustrial expanse of East London in line with the 'rent-seeking impetus of neoliberal urbanism'. Art plays an emollient role, as a 'place holder for national community' (Berry 2015: 87). Our notion of *milieu of labour* allows us to develop an analysis of the streets and neighbourhoods and studio spaces of fashion activity. The *milieu of labour* is an assemblage of various governmental activities; it has the power to make things happen. Specific forms of creative activity can spring into life. Foucault's notion of the milieu as an environmental 'agency' suits our purposes of carrying out research in three cities (London, Berlin and Milan) without the empirical detail that would be required of a full-blown cultural geography[18] and in accordance with Ulrich Beck's (2016) call for sociological research that defines itself 'against methodological nationalism'.

The *milieu of labour* is an activating force. As we will show in Chapter 2 on London, it delegates power to the leading art and design schools, which are then pushed to exert control over space and access to study by means of their 'monopoly rent' status. In Berlin, it oversees a scenario where rents have risen as the city succumbs to the lure of often foreign capital buying into the property market, with any number of battles then ensuing, including, eventually, the introduction and retraction of rent controls.[19] With elements of a residual social democratic polity in place, the *milieu of labour* in Berlin takes shape in a welfare apparatus that takes the form of a (regularly contested and inevitably shrinking) social wage provision. Milan is dominated by family-owned, but now global, fashion companies. Without strong creative industry policy directives from national or regional governments, the *milieu of labour* for small-scale start-up fashion activity takes the form of a city- and nationwide artisanal sensibility dominated by the traditional idea of the family firm. These elements have been pulled together into the widely disseminated idea of 'Made in Italy'. Young people in the city, wanting to take part in the world-leading fashion design scenes, make do without the kinds of urban cultural policy initiatives that would formalize their DIY self-employment fashion practices with a range of state-funded provisions and subsidies. The 'Made in Italy' slogan is a superficial umbrella promoting the idea of craft, artisanship and high-quality design, while the real *milieu of labour* is family, including extended family and community. And the very existence of so many *grandes maisons*, most of which retain the family name of the original owners, from Fendi and Prada to Missoni, Versace and others, produces dense networks of creative sociability and some limited job opportunities in the city neighbourhoods described by Laura Bovone (2006) and Adam Arvidsson and colleagues (2011).

The value of the idea of *milieu of labour* rests on its ability to let us 'follow the actors'. They lead us to their various habitats. The *milieu of labour* provides us with a flow model that recognizes the international aspirations of small-scale fashion endeavours. Two of the Italian respondents, who worked together, yearned to be able to set up a stall in Brick Lane and moved to London a year or so later, eventually returning home to Milan to carry on with their work. Our London key respondents were almost all non-UK nationals, hailing from Brazil, Italy and Finland among other locations. Of course, Brexit throws so much of this kind of activity and planning for futures into disarray. In Berlin, we inter-viewed designers who had trained in London and some who were British but had located to the city. The consultants we interviewed in both Berlin and Milan had spent considerable amounts of time earlier in their careers working in London, one supporting the setting up of the Vivienne Westwood label and another working for a UK textile company.

The *milieu of labour* also holds things together. It manages the movement of bodies, spaces, objects and images. As a research team, we were ourselves both inside and outside the frame of the *milieu of labour*. We also, at points, became enablers, for example when we brought designers from the three cities together for events and workshops, and especially for a two-day group trip to the Glasgow School of Art in Scotland. This provided many opportunities for what policymakers refer to as 'knowledge exchange'; it also gave the designers a chance to make new contacts and pursue new avenues. Each group was interested in the others, as well as in the wider circle of people who attended the Glasgow School of Art afternoon conference.[20] The university or 'art school'

Figures 1–5: CREATe research project, Glasgow School of Art (2016). Photos courtesy of Pau Delgado Iglesias.

Teija Eilola, Marte Hentschel, Esther Perbandt

Esther Perbandt

appears and reappears throughout this study as a kind of anchor. Because almost all designers are undertaking several jobs at a time to supplement the 'own label' work, the idea of teaching in one of the leading art schools is always an attractive option. Drawing attention to the fact that we are inside as well as outside the *milieu of labour* also produces

Chris Brooke, Bruno Bass, Leony Mayhew and Daniel Strutt

a kind of methodological reflexivity. As we became more aware of the struggles faced by the independent designers, as well as the value of not just the work itself, but their overall vision and their social engagement, we often found ourselves becoming advocates for the sector.

Art theory

The neo-Marxist political economy of art theory has significant value for critical fashion studies. Art theory emerged as a form of 'institutional critique' of the dominant art worlds from the late 1980s, where the idea of relational aesthetics provided a forum for an art practice that challenged the fixation on the object and his or her creator, along with the hyper-commercialism of the international art markets (Bourriaud 1998). 'Criticality' was also extended through the writings of Jacques Rancière (where there is a marrying of political philosophy and critical aesthetics) to further consider how art objects circulated in and across so many different public and social locations as 'distributions of the sensible' (see Rancière 2008). From the early 2000s, the neo-Marxism of Michael Hardt and Antonio

Negri brought a further dimension of political theory to the terrain, alongside the writings of other autonomist philosophers such as Paulo Virno, Maurizio Lazzarato and Franco Berardi (see Virno and Hardt 1996; Hardt and Negri 2000; Berardi 2009). Labour re-emerges as a category for renewed political attention. Lazzarato (1996) developed most fully the idea of 'immaterial labour', which in turn was drawn on by various artists to make sense of their own current working practices. Art theory is typically associated with journals such as *Semiotext(e)* and with online magazines such as *e-flux* and *Mute*. Since 2007, following the global financial crisis and new waves of activism and protest movements such as OCCUPY, older feminist artists – for example, Martha Rosler – found themselves resanctified after spending some years in the cold. Overall, art theory has been largely male-dominated and white European in inflection, with artists and theorists of colour only very recently finding a space in this sphere. Most of the activities emanate from university departments and museum and gallery sectors. There is a self-conscious vanguardist radicalism in these anticapitalist initiatives. The rise of art theory as a post-disciplinary practice also reflects the actual growth in the number of young people embarking on careers as artists, including theatre and performance art, computational art, media arts, music-making, spoken word, as well as many other related fields. These same cohorts have participated in protests against gentrification, university fees and the general state of precarization (Lorey 2015). They have made more visible questions of self-exploitation, internships and low pay across the creative sector.

In Kozlowski et al.'s edited volume *Joy Forever* (2013), there is cross-generational dialogue between Martha Rosler ('semiotics of the kitchen') and her younger counterparts. Previous art struggles are recalled, such as Metzger's art strike, described in an article in the same volume by Stevphen Shukaitis titled 'Art Strikes and the Metropolitan Factory'. These pieces, alongside many others, comprise unruly and poetic styles of writing. There is an unwillingness to comply with academic conventions. Referring obliquely and with scepticism to creative economy research, the late German artist Marion von Osten casts doubt on sociological knowledge about artists, in comparison to artists' self-knowledge. She says in interview: 'There are a lot of problems in research when the expertise of the actors in the field is not taken seriously enough. Ethnographical studies are known to be plagued by this. So if it's about creativity, then who are the experts? I guess the artist and the designer' (in von Osten and Barnes 2015).

Talking about a specific project that brought artists and social scientists together, von Osten elaborates on this theme: 'I am not an outsider. I am not an impartial researcher. Coming in and having an object to study. I'm part of the process'. She insists that in the kinds of funded projects that are usually led by social scientists, the artists themselves ought to be in the lead rather than being the object of study. She also implies that artists are privy to the truth of their own experience. Von Osten's interview reveals some of the problems arising from 'post-disciplinarity'. Sociologists conducting research on artists and precarious labour, for example, are required to draw on recognized methodologies that will ensure the investigation is systematic. It is on this inductive and inferential basis that the capacity for concept-making and generalization emerges. What von Osten says is that the insider voice of the artist is more accurate and that post-disciplinary practices produce new conceptual richness in the form of texts, exhibitions and shows.[21] But where we in the social sciences and humanities rely on anonymous peer review as a guide for judging and accrediting our work, in art theory there is a sense that this is not relevant.

A common point of reference across this field of radical art theory is the re-reading of Marx's *Grundrisse* under-taken by autonomist writers (for example, Hardt and Negri 2000), which articulates the surplus of communality (the General Intellect) from worker combination that exceeds the control of the capitalist means of production as it attempts to harness technology and cognitive capacity to its own interests (Marx 1993; Hardt and Negri 2000). This surplus gives rise to 'joyful' resistance and new forms of 'free labour' to be put to oppositional uses (Terranova 2004). More politi-cally optimistic than previous ideology-led Marxisms, and based on an idea of the commons, this suggests a different way of being an artist. There is greater cooperation after decades of competition and naked individualization. This new sense of the commons provides a bridge for art workers stretching from their own practice to that of others, which becomes also a means of understanding their own precarity and a way of developing new experimental modes of political activism, with alliances and action on housing, on financialization and on zero-hours contracts. Here we see a fierce discourse at variance with the governmentality of creativity, the management of populations and the idea of self-entrepreneurialism. Both Lazzarato's theorization of debt as the primary instrument for neoliberal control in financial capitalism and Vishmidt's analysis of how art's autonomy is made to concur with the ethos of speculation in financial capitalism provide the contours for a powerful new political economy (Lazzarato 1996; Vishmidt 2019). These writers extend the remit of art history and political philosophy from a focus on relationality and the critique of the *auteur* to discussions of rent, property and debt and the implications for art in financial capitalism circuits. This proves most helpful to our current study when we reflect in Chapter 2 on the *milieu of labour* in London, where institutional spaces of art and design schools and universities are drawn into the logic of monopoly rent (Moreno 2018a, 2018b).

While no automatic assumptions should be made about direct links between art theory and various forms of artist activism, nevertheless, in some instances, the translation of the concepts into ground-level activity can lead to a naive and ahistorical understanding of social policy issues, including neighbourhood and community politics. Despite good intentions about collaborating with socially excluded people, or those living in poverty or reliant on welfare, artist activists who draw on this vocabulary often show themselves to be unaware of the regulatory frameworks and the ethos of good practice in social policy studies, in youth and community work as well as in antiracist social work (McGarvey 2017). Artists are too ready to take over part of a run-down housing estate with the idea of working with young people, children or the 'local population'. Little attention is given to existing, statutory provision, and to the longstanding local knowledge stored therein. There appears to be little consideration of a dialogue with researchers working in the fields of public policy or criminology.

More generally across this field of debate, the 'object itself' tends to disappear under the waves of, first, institutional critique and then what has come to be known as infrastructural critique (Vishmidt 2009, 2019). The idea is indeed to dethrone the artist as creator while also seemingly abandoning the practice of close textual analysis or readings of objects. When work is referred to, it is often the case that the artist is already part of one or other of the groupings that constitute this new 'commons' and is themself an artist theorist.[22] The danger is that this reduces the potential for wider conversation, becoming instead as hermetic an exchange as was the case in the early days of conceptual art. The art work is deprived of agency, or else it has bad agency. Josephine Berry's (2015) critical description of Anish Kapoor's Orbit Tower in Olympic Park as a tawdry, hollow and branded spectacle, charging its audience for its dubious pleasure, is exemplary for the way in which she embeds her account of the Orbit in the multiple government framings of the milieu, including the disingenuousness of the processes of consultation in decision-making about what might count as public art. But it is more often the case that art theory prefers speculative philosophizing, which, ironically, given the post-disciplinary ethos, confirms a new, and even closed-off, form of canon-making, a new curriculum. This absence of the object also raises a question about the idea of being an artist without producing art works, which could in effect mean not being an artist, but being something else – a curator and organizer, a writer, a philosopher, a social worker, a community organizer, etc. When 'work' that attracts an audience is produced, for example exhibitions, shows or performances, it is often assumed to have the capacity for generating radical counter-knowledge, but this claim generally remains untested. What if the show or performance or exhibition does not live up to the stated aims? What if it falls short? What if it hinders rather than permits 'potential for resistance' (Raunig 2013: 51)?

Fashion and the popular arts have remained largely outside the remit of this body of writing. Presumably this inattention stems from what is perceived from an art theory point of view as the avowedly commercial 'circuit of culture' in which the fashion industry operates, from supply chains to the high street, from magazines to Instagram. Meanwhile, designers trained in fine art fashion have adamantly referred to themselves as artists (see McRobbie 1998; Ugelvig 2020). The marginalization of fashion from the orbit of art theory dates back to the (masculinist) legacy of the Frankfurt School and its influence on critical theory. Fashion in this respect falls under the rubric of mass culture, another form of manipulation of the masses. Despite Walter Benjamin's championing of fashion, a line of negative association can be traced here from Adorno down through various neo-Marxisms (Wollen 2003). And this dismissal is also blind to the writing of many feminist scholars who, from the early 1980s, found good reason to take fashion more seriously (Wilson 1983). Fashion scholarship can benefit from more fruitful exchanges with art theory, albeit from a viewpoint that recognizes the more commercial circuits of culture in which fashion is based. The key rallying point for radical political activity in recent years in fashion has been based on questions of the environment, on sustainability and on exploitation across the supply chains of low-paid workers in countries where labour is cheap. A political agenda has also emerged in fashion that draws attention to the conditions of working for those inside the design companies, from small to large. From the findings of her detailed ethnography of the fashion design workforce in Paris, Giulia Mensitieri paints a picture of rigid hierarchies, substantial amounts of work done without pay, abysmal treatment of freelancers and those working on a subcontractual basis, and a kind of cultish deference to the creative directors and other seemingly charismatic figures who yield all the power (Mensitieri 2021). This focus on the leading brands as places of work, and on the attention it pays to the legions of freelancers and precarious workforces pulled in and pushed out and often not paid at all, raises questions that are relevant to this current study and might also turn out to be a fruitful area of discussion among art theorists. And, as with ideas of immaterial labour, the extractive economy, monopoly rent, debt, speculation, struggle, organization, we can envisage for fashion a more sustained and deeper radicalism – for example the fashion 'commons' and a fashion 'strike'.

The object itself

> The word work and the unity that it designates are probably
> as problematic as the status of the author's individuality.
> (Foucault 1991: 104)

In the chapters that follow, we aim to bring the fashion object
into view, but the question is how? In this respect, Georgina
Born's (2010) call for a 'post-Bourdieusian sociology' of
aesthetics is most promising. She offers a wide interdisciplinary take on the various forces at play in cultural
production, alluding both to the value-attributing powers
of the various forms of media that accompany, guide and
evaluate the objects as they emerge into the daylight, and also
to the pleasure-inducing elements that the object gives to its
designated audiences (and in our case, to consumers, readers,
viewers and 'followers'). Echoing Arjun Appadurai (1988),
Born charts how cultural objects have 'careers' and how they
undergo changes according to the setting in which they make
their various appearances, and this indeed echoes with recent
ideas of circular fashion.[23] She points to the institutional
conditions of possibility, referencing her own ethnographies,
first in the IRCAM Centre and then at the BBC in London.
She retrieves from Bourdieu the tensions that come into play
in his writing between the structuring role of the field and
the habitus of the actors, who are invariably bound by the
competitive dynamics of the field and thus limited in what
they can do. They take up a position and generally stick
with it, acting in a reiterative habitual fashion to meet the
demands of the field (even as it proclaims artistic originality
as a guiding principle). Drawing on postcolonial anthropology, Born argues that it is possible to both investigate the
conditions of possibility that oversee the practices of cultural
producers, while also allocating more space to these 'authorial
subjectivities', such that an analytic might emerge out of a
more dynamic and two-way research process. This would
entail anthropological-empirical work, which departs from
Bourdieu insofar as it would understand art practices in a
performative sense as world-making. Through this move, the
object and its maker are each afforded agency. The cultural

object will change as it circulates; it will also generate many social relations, bringing into play diverse groupings that in turn will perform multiple acts of interpretation and review, such that the work functions as a 'distributional object' while all the time it is aesthetically organized in specific field-related genres. Born provides this persuasive pathway for returning to the object so that it takes its place in contemporary studies of cultural production. She emphasizes the need to account for the full range of institutional conditions of possibility to be understood by means of historical investigation and ethnographic research. It is in these institutional settings that authorial subjectivities shape up. Born's focus of attention with regard to the aesthetic element is the 'genre'. This is what unfolds from the range of organizational discourses at play in the drama department of the BBC. The promise here is that, by understanding the conditions that play a role in shaping what can be created, it becomes possible to think about how, by altering these conditions, different kinds of objects could emerge. In our case of fashion, this might mean, for example, quality, sustainable and circular fashion items that are affordable and aesthetically exciting and appealing to much wider populations of consumers, young and old.

Can we transpose Born's ideas to the fashion objects that are the outcome of our designer's and their team's labours? There are pointers in her account for how analysis of the object from this kind of perspective might proceed. It would mean expanding on the study of the institutional setting by, for example, carrying out ethnographic work in the art and design schools where designers are trained, since this would open up a discussion about fashion design pedagogy and its role in the kind of work that is produced.[24] Likewise, there would be more attention paid to the key policymakers and those who implement and oversee specific initiatives. Paying closer attention to the objects that make up the designer's oeuvre also helps us to better understand their working lives. The object 'speaks' or tells a story, and in so doing allows the researcher to interrogate its movements, to see how it comes together and where it goes. One good example of this narrative agency occurs when a dress or a blouse is worn by a well-known person or celebrity. In the course of our study, and as documented in Chapter 2, a summer dress by one pair of designers (Bruno Basso and Chris Brooke) and a blouse by another (Teija Eilola) were both worn by Michelle Obama, and this created an upsurge almost immediately in orders for these small companies.[25] Here, we would inquire into the qualities of these pieces, their 'genre', and we would seek to understand what made them successful. We would also want to consider the political economy at play, where one single 'hit' and the orders it triggers can have a significant impact on cashflow, albeit over a limited duration, after which it becomes part of the press cuttings. What does it tell us about the commercial world of fashion when this form of instant visibility in a celebrity-driven media format has the power to generate a much-needed income? This is not just a reflection of the power of social media and of Instagram culture, it also reveals new and unfolding relational networks that shortcircuit and eclipse older, slower forms of consumer culture. We would also need to unpack the role of the social media fashion intermediaries who negotiate the pathway for that dress or this blouse to go from the designer atelier into the wardrobe of Michelle Obama, who herself will often be making choices about what kind of fashion culture she wishes to support, including, for example, the work of black and ethnic minority designers.

Looking more closely at the objects also takes us beyond the iterations of fashion labour as 'passionate work'. It is not just in fashion that creative actors will justify the long hours, the low pay and the poor work conditions on the grounds of their own emotional investment in the work. This usually takes the form of an expression of great love for what they are doing. It happens in very many creative professions (Scharff 2017). This ethos is often expressed in autobiographical terms. And for historical and gendered reasons, in fashion this refrain is loud and clear. It can be defensive too, as if to justify what otherwise might look like an endeavour that financially does not add up.[26] Looking more closely at the objects themselves shifts attention to craft and process, to technology and expertise. Such discussions are necessary in this kind of research process. They depend on listening to how the designers talk about what they do on a day-to-day basis and what kind of artistic decisions they are constantly making (see Molotch 2003). Putting the objects (or collections) in this more prominent position permits a better understanding of the circuits of cultural production, and it also brings out the artist in the designer. Finally, it allows the researcher to establish the basis on which he or she might be able to play some kind of advocacy role in whatever shape or form that might take. This leads us to a concluding point concerning the politics of fashion. In the chapters that follow, not only do we pursue these lines of inquiry, with our fashion actors leading us through their own *milieus of labour*, but we also chart, in the course of the writing, a rising tide of wider political awareness, anger and protest as the fashion system per se finds itself in the spotlight of public attention like never before. These campaigns tally with our own efforts here to make the case that fashion can be different and that it can embrace and act on a social justice agenda.

2

London: Independent Fashion and 'Monopoly Rent'

For those of us who believe in the democracy of further education, the new reality of sole domination by upper-class students is a bitter reality to swallow ... In 2016 it's only wealthy people who can afford further education.

(Elan 2016)[1]

Introduction: The 'futures' student as human capital

In this chapter we extend two of the concepts discussed in the previous chapter, 'art theory' and *milieu of labour*. The chapter falls into two main sections. In the first part, we focus on the macroeconomy of land and space and how it connects with the role of the fashion departments in the context of the changes imposed on higher education through what Wendy Brown (2015) refers to as neoliberal rationality. In the second part of the chapter, we present empirical findings from the CREATe project, which entailed conversations, events, trips, studio visits and interviews with thirteen London-based respondents. The key point we make in the first section is that the viability and longevity – and hence success – of London's fashion microenterprises is tied up not only with the seminal role of the leading fashion schools in the city, but increasingly with patterns of land values, monopoly rent and financial capitalism. Housing, work and education form a triage of factors that have created, since the early 2000s, a generational cleavage in the world of independent small-scale fashion design companies. Those who have retained a label and a studio practice of some significance tend to be already in, or are approaching (at the time of writing), their forties, having avoided the full force of 'generation rent'. Those coming up behind them, in their twenties or early thirties, apart from a handful of exceptional prize-winners, have found it almost impossible to juggle the cost of having their own studio space with finding a place to live. This accounts for our focus in the second part of the chapter on an older cohort of established independent designers. It seems that younger graduates are nowadays more likely to look for jobs as junior design assistants in a range of London companies rather than aim to develop their 'own label' work.

Our investigations look at how fashion designers work in an independent capacity in London, a city known across the world for training highly experimental artist designers, most of whom have also imbued the spirit of working-class subcultural Britain alongside the history of pop culture. And this requires nowadays an engagement with matters of political economy, especially regarding space, property and land value. We are forced into considering London's skyline. There is no shying away from the reality of financial capitalism and how it encroaches on and limits the ability of this strata of creative workers to pursue their chosen careers. We find ourselves plunging into questions of real estate and the asset-stripping of publicly owned land and buildings. London has become 'lifted out' from the prevailing economic structures that define British society, and its leading art and design universities have become 'super brands' and hence also 'lifted out' from the ordinary everyday economy (Giddens 1998). The complex tools of currency trading and algorithmic systems that come into being around the dominance of the financial sector shape the wider cultural landscape as well as the possibilities for livelihoods in the creative economy (Harvey 2001; Moreno 2014). London is not just 'lifted out', it floats high up in the stratosphere, having produced an economy of winners-take-all, leaving the regions below, the other big cities, and the entire UK apart from the South-East, scrabbling to create different local economies. As a recent report shows, London and the South-East taken together constitute 57 per cent of all fashion economic activity (Harris et al. 2021).

The space–power axis of London creates often insurmountable difficulties for young people because of escalations in land values and 'monopoly rent'. Nowadays only young people with independent wealth (or at least with parents willing to support them) can embark on a career as an independent designer, especially since they may already be up to £50,000 in debt having taken out student loans to cover their fees and living costs during their undergraduate years (Banks and Oakley 2016; Elan 2016). (For international graduates, the debt mountain and overall costs will be a lot higher.) And the handful of annual prize-winners, if they come from modest backgrounds, must seek out accelerated, indeed frenetic and multitasking, ways of getting an income. Inside the universities, one of the cruel outcomes of the current configuration of the *milieu of labour* is that new developments, including spacious and interesting modern buildings for teaching fashion design (among other fashion-related subjects), can only be realized in the futures-based portfolio assets and coffers of property developers and the formulas of public–private partnerships.[2] Low-income students can barely afford to live and work in proximity to these dazzling campuses without taking on substantial debt. They are therefore subjects of a 'risk society' (Beck 1986). They must calculate, along with their parents, whether they can rely on a 'return on investment' (ROI). Will their individual talent as human capital reap the rewards? For many aspiring fashion students, especially from working-class and ethnic minority backgrounds, this a calculation too far, which in turn makes the neoliberal education system one of increasing inequalities. University managers defend their decisions by arguing that only by entering into long-term borrowing arrangements, while also selling off at least some of the university-owned land and buildings, can they improve and update the infrastructure for their higher education provision. And then, to service the loans, they need to attract wealthy international students able to pay not just tuition fees, but also expensive, even luxury, accommodation, which has often been built as part of the same portfolio regeneration plans that permitted the improvements to the basic infrastructure in the first place – for example, new lecture theatres, cafés, libraries and digital hub spaces, etc.[3] Students are thus captured in a portfolio of futures assets.

Some of these well-off students may also be able to stay on after graduation and can afford the kind of studio spaces that are springing up but would be well beyond the means of those without a private source of funds. And so, despite many official statements about widening the social net of participation for this kind of university education to include young people from poor families, and especially from ethnic minorities, it is fees, alongside living and working spaces, that thwart this ambition.[4] This leads to an unsatisfactory as well as an unsettling situation. Why? Because ideas about (albeit well-off) 'foreign students' also give rise to both old and new racisms and colonial prejudices.[5] As Anna Minton points out, 'student accommodation in London is the most expensive in the world', with only the children of the rich being able to afford monthly rents of over £900 (2017: 43).[6] Minton also quotes the upmarket estate agent Savills on the 'flowering of student housing' in the city as a 'global asset class'. Student rents promise high returns on property investment, making this social group a key factor in the 'growth machine'.[7] London is no longer affordable for young creative people from working-class backgrounds who, in the not so distant past, had been able to make a decisive and significant contribution to the arts and culture. Some of the designers who took part in our CREATe study were forced to leave London for Margate, or they stayed on and set up a business by 'sofa surfing' for months on end. Others moved to Berlin or Lisbon, unable to afford London rents or keep up with mortgage repayments as well as run a business. Later in this section, we point to developments (post-2016) at Hackney Wick Fish Island (HWFI) close to Stratford and Olympic Park, where, by 2023, the London College of Fashion (LCF) will have moved its entire campus. The HWFI project of fashion studio spaces is overseen by the Trampery, a UK social enterprise that, in 2009, set up a large co-working space opposite the Centre for Fashion Enterprise in Mare Street, Hackney, but which shut its doors in 2013 as a result of exponential rent rises.

David Harvey, Louis Moreno and others have provided compelling accounts of some of the factors that have impinged on the livelihoods of the creative workers we are considering here (Harvey 2001, 2008; Moreno 2014). Through the vast reserves of pension monies and other resources of wealth generated from mortgages, insurance services and private equity hedge funds, the City of London can offer long-term loans at seemingly low interest rates to the public sector. Higher education is attractive to lenders because of its direct connection with one reliable asset; namely, youth and future generations as human capital. Space and the skyline are at the centre of these activities, which became dominant in the 2000s and then accelerated after the banking and financial crisis of 2007/8. This heralds a new age of finance capitalism beyond post-Fordism. This neoliberal regime can also dispense with the need for an expanding labour force; indeed, it makes logical sense to reduce the number of employees since they always entail some degree of legal and welfare provisions. The profit is now instead from 'extractive' rent and from the servicing of debt. With fewer obligations to a workforce, this new capitalism merely oversees at the lower end a sprawling 'disorganized' service sector (Sassen 1991). There are parallels here with the fate of the workforce inside universities. Teachers and lecturers have also been subject to extensive casualization and short-term contracts. In addition, the young urban creative workforce has, since the early 2000s, been a prime subject of the creativity *dispositif*. What is dangled in front of the eyes of these workers are the rewards of self-expressive work in the 'talent-led economy', but, being self-employed, they must, of course, forgo the protections of traditional employment, from sick pay to maternity leave, etc. (McRobbie 2016).[8] These precarious populations now live side by side in London's inner-city locations.[9] Finance capitalism can operate without having to make such large investments in labour, since so much of the profit is rents-based. As is well documented, there has been extensive wage stagnation and, overall, a degradation of labour. And younger creative cohorts, unless they have private resources, are increasingly pushed out, their livelihoods threatened due to the high cost of rent. It is for this reason that the research findings we describe below are heavily weighted by generation. When we focus on the period of our study, it becomes apparent that 'urban space has become an integrated platform through which finance-capital is geographically concentrated and specialized' (Moreno 2014: 264).

From the new King's Cross to Hackney Wick Fish Island

So far, we have indicated the way in which housing and higher education in London are part of the neoliberal rationality where market values take precedence and where finance and debt are embedded features of day-to-day processes of governance in the form of student loans, home loans and rent. We have also seen how this equates with intensifying inequality. The key sites for fashion education and pedagogy in London, namely Central Saint Martins (CSM) and the LCF, are institutions of higher education (part of the University of the Arts London) that have been entangled and caught up in these processes of urban development on a grand scale. This happened first in the old King's Cross area, where a massive expanse of disused railways buildings was transformed into a glittering canal-side campus. CSM was the first tenant and occupied a huge space designed with the aim of increasing the number of students enrolled in a variety of degree courses. This was followed, as described by Moreno (2018a), by the more recent expansion of an upmarket leisure and retail complex along Coal Drops Yard, as well as a huge housing complex designed for wealthy tenants and owners that extends right up to the end of York Way, where a run-down housing Camden Council estate has been largely replaced by new apartment developments. The presence of both Facebook and Google headquarters, each bringing in their own upmarket workforce with high spending power, created the incentive for the opening of many bars and restaurants, so that the whole neighbourhood became a new leisure zone as well as a residential quarter. In the space of less than a decade, it has come to resemble a mini-Manhattan. This started with the sale of public-owned land for £371 million to the property developer company Argent, to accommodate these new buildings and to expedite the transformation of King's Cross into a highly attractive neighbourhood for a predominantly well-off and professional population.[10] Under the new finance capital arrangements, as it replaces the traditional role of the local authority, a 'social' function has to become part of the property development process. Various experts, from architects to planners and cultural geographers, have judged the renovations of the sixty-seven acres of Kings Cross to be remarkably successful, an 'exemplary urban development' and a 'compact, resource-efficient and "liveable" global city model' (Adelfio et al. 2020).

Spotlighting multi-use open-air spaces and high environmental standards, these commentaries pay less attention to the socioeconomic issues relating to housing, education and public and community provision; noticeably missing is any focus on the importance of space for living and for social reproduction for a wider section of the population (in the form of leisure and community facilities). Instead, the consensus seems to be that the planning and design of the whole terrain constitutes 'good practice' (Adelfio et al. 2020). Moreno (2018b) argues that the character of the new neighbourhood displays features that are more sensitive to public needs than might otherwise be expected from a private big capital investment.[11] But these seem more like gestures community-building by the developers of the privately owned spaces (with their cathedral-like ceilings, chandeliers and concierges) and their preferred upmarket visitors who will enjoy the public leisure walkways, such as the canal-side area and the various pedestrian paths leading from King's Cross and St Pancras Stations to the shops, bars and restaurants and the Waitrose supermarket (formerly a tram shed). Beyond these are more glamourous apartments for a 'high net worth individual' clientele. The pinnacle of these new homes comprises the circular penthouse apartments set within iron frames of the old gasometers. They give way to what seem to be lavishly equipped 'luxury' student accommodation alongside more private flats stretching right up to the top of York Way. There is an even higher density of units as more buildings appear from month to month, including during the pandemic of 2020–22, some with a range of sparkling architectural features (a white crochet-like texture on the building fronts), presumably again to attract a cognoscenti of well-off tenants or buyers. As any casual walk or stroll in the new neighbourhood will show, the population is startlingly homogenous; there are very few old people, only small clusters of children with their parents, an atmosphere of affluent multiculturalism, and no sign whatsoever of a working-class London population.

With the reduction of publicly owned land as a result of sell-offs by local councils, and a demise in the urban welfare apparatus, finance capital must, no matter how reluctantly, pick up a role as 'provider'. The social and environmental responsibility mandate (usually written into contracts and tenders) means that it must manage a repertoire of public functions, many of which are adjusted and shrunken in scale as time passes.[12] Neoliberal governance is now charged with the role of overseeing 'the social'. What is the future of welfare and social security (in the form of housing, education and training in our case) when neoliberalism is so pervasively entrenched, and resistant to the whole idea of welfare? When this power over land and space and public facilities reaches down into the classrooms and lecture theatres, what is the outcome on a day-to-day basis? This marks a new unfolding of the logic of neoliberalism into the nexus of creative economy activity, through urban space and on into the day-to-day functioning of universities. If anti-welfarism was a key component of the first decade of the twenty-first century in the UK, coinciding as that period did with the financial crisis of 2008, what kind of obligation do these forces now find themselves burdened with in the spheres of social reproduction? In London at that time there was little in the way of organized opposition, which accounts for the ease with which rents rose exponentially. People were displaced and the student fee system, though meeting resistance, was implemented as part of the new financial regime of loans and debts. The early years of the creative class 'hipster' euphoria conveniently masked the deeper restructuring that was to produce profound polariz-ations of wealth and poverty in London as well as across the UK (McRobbie 2016).

Just as the King's Cross neighbourhood has come to exemplify a neoliberal finance-led governance of space, with 'the social' in the form of higher education being prominent as an instrument for the growth machine, so also do we find a distinctive kind of rhetoric emerge in relation to the equally expansive plans for Olympic Park, extending to the Hackney Wick Fish Island area (Wainwright 2022). The London College of Fashion, along with a few departments from University College London, is moving in its entirety to this new site in 2023.[13] Called the 'Fashion District at the East Bank', a key feature of this extensive development is its promise to deliver culture, education and social value in the form of local employment. Located in an area that had been underused until the 2012 Olympics and the development of the large Westfields shopping mall at Stratford, along with the gleaming new train station and Eurostar terminus, the overall vision on the part of the planners and developers has been to open up to the global economy this part of east London that is more often associated with wasteland, warehouses and distribution and fulfilment centres. However, the area was not more or less empty of inhabitants, but was instead surrounded by dense working-class housing and areas of historic deprivation. Hackney Wick was home also to various small businesses that were priced out of the neighbourhood to make way for glamourous new-build apartments. The social or public function is again marked by the appearance in the neighbourhood of a world-leading fashion college and other universities, and they in turn are charged with overseeing what are nebulously defined as job-creation projects in the local community.[14] With higher education facilities come housing and more luxury student accommodation.[15] Students become the prime subjects of extractive capitalism. Their presence becomes part of a developer's planning ambitions for housing that offers good return on investment. At the time of writing, in Hackney Wick, as in King's Cross, new residential blocks are shooting up. One bedroom 'new builds' at Fish Island Village are advertised for sale at £495,00 with the caption 'Help to buy' running along the bottom of the artfully shot photographs.[16] This is one of the logics of the original creative economy discourse. There is, as David Harvey (2002) has put it, 'accumulation through dispossession'.

The word gentrification does not begin to account for the complexity and scale of the kind of undertaking at King's Cross and, more recently, at HWFI, both of which rely on a magnet effect for various global companies and mega-corporations to establish new headquarters in these now inviting new 'urban glamour zones' (Sassen 2002).[17] In King's Cross, this includes Google and Universal Music, as well as Facebook and YouTube, all companies that rely on an image of youthful energy and excitement. Harvey (2002) refers to this kind of process as the 'art of rent' dedicated to producing a 'growth machine'. These concepts provide us with an analytic for understanding the space–time dynamics that come into play in the 'fashion formations' that have emerged in the city over the past two decades (Casadei et al. 2020). They help us to see how financial capitalism touches down and shapes the cultural life of the city. The banking system and finance economy in London exert enormous power and influence over the spaces where people can live and work. From penthouse suites and gated communities with gyms and mid-air-suspended swimming pools (as in the new Nine Elms development at Vauxhall) for 'high net worth individuals', to the new build-to-rent developments that are still too expensive for average income public sector workers, to the sink estates for the low-paid service class, this all amounts to the 'institutionalization of rent' as London becomes a 'spatial product' where the 'centralization and concentration of urban value is socially constructed' (Moreno 2018b: 158).[18]

The *milieu of labour*: London

Fashion in terms of a place of work does not surface in the reports emanating from the British Fashion Council (or the newly established Fashion Roundtable[19]), and it is only very recently, as a result of student-led activism, that academics have begun to take notice of the new more politicized vocabularies in circulation about work, employment and precarity.[20] There remain the entrenched power and allure of fashion's consumer culture and the presence of the world-leading brands and the fashion media, so much so that these are interwoven as if to present a seamless public image, a glamorous billboard effect.[21] Now sitting at the heart of two 'urban glamour zones', the two constituent colleges of the University of the Arts (CSM and LCF) comprise the dominant *milieu of fashion labour* in London (Sassen 2002). The historic role they have played in the British fashion industry as the leading centres for education and training means that they have been, and remain, nodal points for professionals in the field as well as for journalists and editors, leading retailers and policymakers in the creative economy. This is where the distinctive subjectivities of the 'star' or *auteur* designer are shaped through the range of pedagogies in place. These colleges seem to be almost unassailable in their role as agents of distribution for the various fashion labour markets. Doors are opened to a CV that shows graduation from CSM, or a letter of recommendation from one of the heads of the fashion departments. This mode of 'pedagogic governance' typically operates with a circular call-back function so that prize-winning students who go on to have a glossy career will often return some years later as tutors.

Because of these colleges' long-established connections with a large range of textile and technology firms, and also with the big fashion design companies, it is relatively easy for them to introduce business school thinking directly into this pedagogic environment.[22] The two main London schools are therefore able to fully exploit their position as super-brands in the reputation economy. The fashion media refers to this legacy of success in an almost ritualistic way. Stories of stardom (from Stella McCartney to Alexander McQueen, Christopher Kane and, more recently, J. W. Anderson, Jonathan Saunders, Grace Wales Bonner and others) acquire a mythical status, and students from all over the world compete for places. Recruitment is secured for the purposes of cashflow and future borrowing. Fashion pedagogy functions then in an environment that has been overseen from a distance by the forces of finance-led developments like that in the King's Cross neighbourhood and in the new Olympic Park, which is still being developed. Fashion education and consumer culture create a dream landscape for new styles of living for those able to afford the housing developments and expensive shops. Universities and local councils need to generate funds through a 'mesh of intra-financial claims and obligations' (Adair Turner, quoted by Moreno 2014: 260).

The financialization of the urban process shapes the changing skyline of London and, in doing so, it can extract even further value from these world-leading institutions in the form of upmarket property development.[23] Higher returns of social capital are to be gained by purchasers from having a top-rated university on their doorsteps. Education and learning are instrumentalized to become part of the asset mentality of the property portfolio logic. For decades, an artist population has been used by property developers as a temporary way of making a run-down area attractive, while also pushing out those populations deemed too poor to bring any value to the locations (Zukin 1989). Nowadays, it is students who are designated as a population for the extraction of value on a projected futures market, since universities can make assumptions about their ability to recruit year in, year out. In our case, this student body is destined also to become part of a professional creative sector, itself a terrain of precarious careers, hence the higher level of risk involved in the debt burden. For determined students from low-income families who have dreamt of a place in one of these prestigious institutions, the risk factor is high across all levels of their everyday life: from rent to transport, from the cost of keeping up a social life with fellow students from much higher income brackets, to the need to take on jobs during term time, which means less time for studying and possibly a less stellar outcome. Typically described as exciting developments by university managers, with the promise of growth in these competitive environments, and increasingly reliant on fees paid by overseas students, this 'monopoly rent' strategy, which hinges round the reputation economy, has become a kind of golden gateway to expansion and success in higher education.[24] This amounts to a 'neo-rentier grab for basic infrastructure as part of the overall asset stripping of [public resources]' (Hudson 2013, quoted in Moreno 2014: 260). The ethos of competition and the audit culture and ratings systems so embedded in the UK higher education system mean that the London fashion colleges attract more than their fair share of publicity and media attention. They can afford glossy brochures and can brand themselves on the basis of the names of their prize-winning graduates. Their success becomes a self-fulfilling prophecy, which inevitably drains other fashion departments of resources and makes them seem more drab and provincial. This in turn is another way of compounding inequalities.

Fashion independents: Making a living

In this section, our attention turns to the working lives of the independent fashion designers who took part in this study. We met up with all of them on countless occasions and continued to follow their career pathways well after the formal conclusion of the research project. (The size of the cohort expanded to include a few one-off sessions with designers such as Margaret Howell, and on two occasions we invited younger designers to give talks to undergraduates and postgraduates at Goldsmiths.) The tighter group, however, fell into two subgroupings. There were the fashion design professionals, who had their own studio practices even though these were not always their main or sole source of income, and then there was a group of four 'star' designers. We wanted to find out about their working lives, the access they had to space and how the work itself (the material objects) shaped their different career pathways. Various theorists of neoliberalism have pointed to the Silicon Valley-style social network as the mechanism for maintaining and renewing the human capital quotient. However, in this sector, known for its precarity and also for the need of many to supplement their own label with freelance work, it seemed that this network space had been repurposed. Some people might be working for high street brands, such as Jigsaw or Whistles, while others reached senior positions with star designers, but were suddenly sacked. Overall, there was less snobbishness and more awareness of the pitfalls of the sector at every level. (This marks London out from Paris: see Mensitieri 2021.) The working culture we observed reflected the past times of being a student and partying, with London's subcultural history and multicultural identity encouraging an open-mindedness and questioning of authority. The fashion scene, including magazines like *iD*, had fostered this liberal and egalitarian ethos. The designers were all outward-looking and public-minded; they were less enamoured of the mystique of the business, less impressed by the culture of *Vogue* magazine or the British Fashion Council and more practical about their careers, aware of all the downsides. The *milieu of labour* for this generational cohort marginally less affected by the recent exponential rises in rent for studio space in London had therefore enabled a confident professional outlook. Almost everyone had done some amount of tutoring in the art and design departments from which they had graduated, and they felt themselves to be part of the independent London fashion scene.

Many of the themes discussed so far were reiterated across the interviews and discussions we held with the designer participants. They found full expression when we invited respondents to give short talks at the seminars and workshops we organized in various locations, from Milan University to the Glasgow School of Art to the British Council in Berlin. These perspectives can be summarized in the brief portraits presented below of three designers: Kenneth Mackenzie, Rose Sinclair and Christine Checinska. What emerges, not surprisingly, is that it is the object, the collection and the actual specialism that drive career pathways. The techniques, mechanics and oeuvre of one's 'own work', including style and aesthetics, and hence the wider cultural meaning of the work and the world it opens up to, shape the possible directions for collaborations, for entirely new options, and for opportunities – for example, in teaching. In sociological terms, there is an unfolding, a constantly evolving practice.

Kenneth Mackenzie's menswear label 6876 is based in his Brunswick Centre studio space in Bloomsbury, also, as it happens, a remnant from the Greater London Council (GLC)[25] days, when affordable, dedicated work spaces were made available for rent to small-scale creative enterprises in fashion and related activities. Mackenzie's studio is in the architecturally award-winning development that is now managed by Camden Council. Our visit revealed plenty of room to store large box files full of archive materials and press cuttings, as well as room for rails of clothes from the new collection, and enough space for an intern and an assistant to work at their desks. Having this space was vital to the survival of Mackenzie's label since this was a one-person menswear line in a highly competitive field.

As Mackenzie said in the course of our discussion: 'At the moment in London there is no incentive for fashion start-ups, the costs are prohibitive ... There is a lack of government support. Despite the talk about regenerating manufacture, the only place you see people working on looms or weaving is in the art schools.'

Mackenzie's work is driven by a love of British youth culture, especially the Mod style of the 1960s and also the working-class casuals and football styles that he has cross-fertilized with the sophisticated masculinity of French cinema of the late 1960s. The British Mods admired Italian masculine tailoring and razor-sharp suits (Hebdige 1978). The new wave of French cinema in the 1960s celebrated an urban flamboyance in men's fashion in contrast to the drabness of what came before. Mackenzie enjoys dropping in references to French cultural theory in his press material, such as the idea of the *dérive* (from the Situationists in Paris in the late 1960s), which he playfully uses to explain his concept for socks.[26] This genre of work is produced using top-quality fabrics often in subtle and unusual colours. There are high levels of craftsmanship in the manufacturing, and the collections are presented in striking visual images across Facebook and Instagram. There is an interesting reworking of masculinity that is doubtless appealing to the high street companies and that can, of course, be copied and produced with inferior fabrics at cheaper prices. It is therefore a tough job balancing the books and staying ahead for such a small-scale operation.

Rose Sinclair, one of two black British fashion and textile designers who joined our research, graduated from CSM and then opted for secondary school teaching rather than the perilous pathway to self-employment. Later, she gravitated towards university teaching and completed her PhD at Goldsmiths while all the time maintaining her own small studio practice, as well as writing key textbooks on textile theory and practice.[27] As an exemplary multitasker, Sinclair has been at the forefront of the move to foreground black creative practice, with her work on the Dorcas craft circles now attracting a good deal of attention. Most recently, she co-curated the first ever exhibition on the work of Althea McNish at the William Morris Gallery in Walthamstow, in north-east London. McNish was a pioneering textile designer whose work is only now being recognized. In all the discussions for the CREATe project and in her talk delivered at the British Council in Berlin for CREATe, Sinclair made the point strongly that affordable studio space and access to the right equipment were vital for design practitioners. Some years earlier, she did not attempt to look for studio space in inner London, and instead found cheaper office space in an underused 1960s block near to where she lived in the suburbs of south London: 'For young designers now, the cost of the right technology and software is prohibitive, then getting that insured if it's kept in a studio even more. I got interested in the technology early on and I now have £40,000 worth in the secure office space I work from, near to my home' (interview, 2016).

For Rose Sinclair and for our other black British respondent Christine Checinska, the politics of space and the money needed to embark on an independent practice are amplified through the prism of race and their experience of racism in fashion. Both women made the point that for people from middle- to low-income ethnic minority families the idea of starting up in fashion has been traditionally discouraged because of its unreliable financial rewards, and so they have both chosen a careful pathway; Checinska, for example, turned down a place on the prestigious Master's programme at CSM in favour of a more immediate job, though, as she said, working for Topshop provided her with a wealth of experience.

> I left art school with an offer of a place on the MA at CSM, but I wanted to earn money so I took a job at the Burton Group (including Topshop). Right from the start we were given free range, there was a large design team and in many ways it was like being back at art school, but we also learnt a lot more about the business. We were encouraged to use our imaginations and show our work. We did our research, we went to look at exhibitions, and all the things you do while you are studying. (Interview, March 2016)

After Topshop, Checinska gained more experience right across the sector, first with Laura Ashley and then moving to a more senior role at Margaret Howell. When the company was being restructured, she decided to study for a PhD at Goldsmiths; she had a steady flow of freelance work as well as her own studio work during this time. Checinska's PhD thesis was on the dress styles of Caribbean young men as they arrived in the UK as part of the Windrush generation in the 1950s. Checinska, like Rose Sinclair, has also, over the years, developed a curatorial practice; in 2021 she was appointed Senior Curator of African and African Diaspora Fashion at the Victoria and Albert Museum in London, with a major show in 2022.

These two black women designers demonstrate clearly the energy and steadfastness needed to overcome racism in the sector and to maintain faith in their personal visions and in their political commitment to see the work of other historically marginalized black designers awarded their place in history. They both understood early on the need for dedicated space and for multiple sources of income, with educational institutions and, increasingly, the gallery system providing at least some economic security.

The precarity of success?

I had been on maternity leave after five years with Ted Baker and I thought this is the time to see if I can set up my own label. I had just three weeks to apply for a place as part of the Fashion Fringe/Colin McDowell Programme and be accepted onto their programme. I had to develop a full business plan almost on the spot. To get a place you have to be one of the three chosen from so many, I didn't win the first prize but I was among the first three and I could not believe it when I got a call from Christopher Bailey [of Burberry] inviting me in for a meeting. (Teija Eilola, interview 2016)

Teija Eilola, originally from Finland, graduated from the Royal College of Art (RCA) and then followed a pathway into setting up her own label having accumulated many contacts during the five years she spent working in the youth culture high street brand Ted Baker. Her timing for launching her own label kept her within range of still being a recent graduate and thus counting as youthful talent, an important marker in the competitive stakes. The programme that supported her helped her to find a studio space in an off-street former warehouse in Highbury, Islington, converted for small creative businesses. The Screenworks premises is a co-working space offering a restaurant and coffee area quiet enough for private business conversation, with the studios upstairs. Eilola said that it was a small space, but that she managed to cram everything in, including, when needed, her pattern cutter and an intern assistant. Alongside this working space, she was also offered intensive mentoring as part of the award, as well as introductions to key players who, in turn, helped her to gain access to London Fashion Week and to key Paris fashion agents. The portfolio that she has been able to establish since setting up includes a strong connection with high-end French boutiques, a prestigious slot in Dover Street Market in London, a showing at London Fashion Week, a good deal of press and publicity and having one of her blouses worn by Michelle Obama. These are all indicators of the 'high-end' market. In 2016, Eilola's working life revolved around the home she shared with her husband in Muswell Hill, the studio in Islington, the central London locations for shows, and trips to Paris to be updated on her sales in France.[28]

> London is my base and it's great for dealing with France. An agent approached me and I have been working with her ever since ... My influences are Finland and Japan (Rei Kawakuba minimalism with a peasant touch). This was developed during my time at the RCA. My work and my career are right now moving fast ... there are orders coming in and so many buyers coming to the showrooms. I spend time with every single one and there is a lot of interest from Japan. Sometimes the buyers want a button changed here or there. Or they say what could be different. But I know why every detail is there. (Interview, 2016)

Eilola's collections have found their customer base in upmarket boutiques across the world. To start with, the most interest came from Paris and then from outlets in other

French towns and cities. The taste frames of well-off French young women match well with this aesthetic. It suggests a Jil Sander-influenced minimalism of clean cuts and simple wide styles of trousers, coats, dresses and blouses. There are references to Japanese designers (Kawakuba, Miyake) in the repeated use of triangular and tubular silhouettes, but with unexpected sequences of embroidery and smocking. The Nordic severity of the crisp cottons is offset by this detail, with a palette of low-key greys, pale blues, whites, black, mustards and beiges. The prices are high (approximately £350 for a blouse in 2022) and the items are chic and understated. Eilola is a good example of the independent, highly regarded, prize-winning, UK-trained fashion designer. When we first met, she was working on a low investment basis, her team was small and she pulled in assistants on a freelance basis when needed. Her years at Ted Baker had given her a wide knowledge base about manufacture and production and she drew on this to find the right factories for her orders. 'At the moment it is Lithuania, I don't have time to visit the factories but it can all be done by phone and email. The cotton comes from Switzerland, Italy and France the best quality available and I then add to this the Indian embroidery' (personal interview, 2016).

It is also easy to see how mid-market companies would copy these designs (with sufficient vagueness to avoid infringement of intellectual property) and find ways of producing much cheaper versions. Eilola's summer blouses of 2017/18 were widely copied by fast fashion companies, and consequently worn by young women across the length and breadth of the UK for more than one season. The publicity value of having a blouse worn by Michelle Obama put her even more firmly on the map, leading to offers from high street brands for more lucrative collaborations.

Eilola proved to be one of the designers most interested in participating in the CREATe research project. She joined the team for two key events in the research cycle: the trip to Glasgow School of Art in May 2016, where she gave a talk in the half-day conference, and the evening event hosted at the Royal Society for the Arts in London's Covent Garden, where she took part in the vernissage for the project. Like everyone else we interviewed, she expressed strongly the need for better policymaking for the sector. At both events, Eilola drew attention to the needs of younger fashion designers to be able to access the basic requirements for a successful practice in the UK. She drew attention to the high cost of rentable space and the difficulties involved when companies like hers began to expand. Eilola was looking for leadership in a new vein and separate from the old model adhered to by the British Fashion Council. This led her in the direction of understanding fashion as a creative industry, and as a force that connected with wider social and cultural issues. Her training in the fine art tradition of fashion at the RCA gave her a strong professional identity. From her start-up days in 2012, she had a strong vision of where she could take her work, partly also through her knowledge of the terrain and the extent to which she was plugged into the kind of network sociality referred to in the earlier section of this chapter. The success she has had with her label so far is fully in line with the facilitating function of London's art school ethos and its function as a *milieu of labour* for the fashion industry in the UK.

Moving to Cornwall during the Covid-19 pandemic suggests what Ulrich Beck, in his writing on 'abnormal work', described as a biographical solution to a range of structural problems that, in this case, both pre-date the pandemic (cost of space, cost of childcare) and were then highlighted and exacerbated by the pandemic, with the sudden downturn, if not collapse, in consumer culture. A move like this was more viable because of accumulated credits in the fashion reputation economy (Arvidsson and Pietersen 2013). A steady stream of awards, prizes and other forms of recognition, alongside regular coverage across the fashion media, means that Eilola's work is established in the high-end luxury market and with wide international appeal. The changes since 2020 have led to a lot of adjustment, to introduce a made-to-order system (and thus save on unsold stock), to develop techniques based on more natural, less harmful raw materials, to devise ways of using old and used fabrics and, at the same time, to recalibrate the whole undertaking for online promotion of the work, and for online sales. Even more daunting have been the hurdles posed by Brexit, especially around the movement of goods and the high costs that this now entails. These various demands, which require both expertise and knowledge across many areas, as well as the need to employ different people in a new capacity while, at the same time, keeping up a public profile to ensure possible collaborations with bigger companies even as new collections are being planned, indicate the scale of the pressure. Of our cohort of prize-winners, Eilola remains the most consistent and stable in her success. But she cannot take her foot off the pedal because retaining an *auteur* identity in fashion (as in the creative industries as a whole) rests not just on the creative vision of the designer, but also on her ability to remain visible in and across this commercial sector as it confronts criticism on an unparalleled basis, and as it faces the downturn in customer spending that started during the pandemic and is likely to continue. This is more burdensome for designers without the backing of one of the major *maisons* or their financier companies. Recognition of fashion's place in the creative economy discourses partly accrued through her involvement in the CREATe project made it easier for Eilola to establish an identity in Cornwall.

> I have three organizations who are able to offer the label small grants as part of Cornwall-focused business developments. There is huge amount of 'Creative Industries in Cornwall' projects/support hubs etc. happening. I was invited to apply to be on a small course to be trained in creative leadership in Cornwall (maybe 8 zoom sessions etc.).
>
> You can seek to be an ambassador of creative industries in Cornwall after it. Not sure what it entails, but these are all projects that interest me. Especially if there are some community/innovation/sustainability or supporting small creative labels angles to them. (Email, 3 May 2021)

Carlo Volpi is another prize-winning designer who played an active role in the study. During this whole period, he was commuting on budget airlines almost weekly between London and Milan. A native Italian from Florence, now in his late thirties, he followed a pathway from a BA at Goldsmiths to the RCA and, after that, won various prizes and accolades as well as features in *Vogue Italia*.[29] Specializing in avant-garde knitwear, but with an equally strong craft element, it was this mix that qualified him to apply to, and then get an interview for, the craft-based studio space Cockpit Arts in Holborn, London. 'I got the Cockpit Space free for a year and I'm still here several years later. But I'm not living off my own brand, I need to do a million jobs to support myself, to keep going.'[30] Having this space proved to be the decisive factor for Volpi in that it allowed him to maintain his own label, without having to face huge and unaffordable rent costs. He was offered work experience while studying for his Master's at RCA and, following graduation, this led to well-paid work with the same Italian company. He found work by this university-based route with three different companies in Italy, all of which looked to the RCA as a major training institution for conceptual fashion. Volpi's adventurous stance appealed to the more conservative Italian companies. 'I wanted to take the piss out of menswear. I was listening all the time to BBC Radio 2 aiming to get inspiration from something really obvious. I don't see myself as an Italian designer, more like an old-fashioned British designer. I like the idea of having some poison in my work ... Its not money oriented, it's the idea' (interview, February 2016).

After getting his MA, Volpi was offered teaching on various BA courses. 'The main thing that came out of the Master's course was that I was offered some regular teaching, back at Goldsmiths and also at the RCA.' This range of possibilities in itself demonstrates the role of the art and design schools as *milieus of labour*, which in Volpi's case enabled him to forge a career pathway and a professional identity as a designer. From that point onwards, he was able to start selling pieces to niche upmarket design spaces such as Darkroom in Holborn as well as through the more mainstream Wolf and Badger, while also trying to find the right way to connect with large fashion shops like Selfridges in between his regular commutes from Italy to the UK, often touching down in London just for his teaching hours.

> I've started my own brand business all on my own. At the time I didn't have a studio and I wasn't really thinking about having my own business. I thought I would just do my own collection and put it out there. It took me a long time in between all my other jobs to actually have the time to make it

work. But I put it online and almost immediately it got picked up by Italian *Vogue* and they are still supporting me, and that is why I keep going. I've been doing my collections since then. (Interview, February 2016)

In every way, and prior to the pandemic, Volpi epitomizes the 'precarity of success'. 'The scarves are made by a lady in southern Italy, not in a factory. I met her on Facebook in a knitting group ... I send her one sample, all the yarn and instructions and she does a run of about fifty for me. I do all of the more complicated stuff myself' (interview, February 2016).

Conceptual knitwear, mostly for men, but with a strong gender-neutral dimension, does indeed reflect the British art school subcultural and subversive tradition from the punk and post-punk period. The breakthrough here to the Italian and typically conservative menswear market was key to Volpi's success. His knitwear breaks all the rules; the work has a three-dimensional sculptural form, and this is what attracted the attention of *Vogue* magazine. He also brings knitwear into club culture spaces, working against the usual body-skimming shapes in favour or large and baggy voluminous styles. He uses dazzling electric colours and garments from which strange protuberances and horticultural shapes seem to grow. In one collection the model was encased in a heavy-hanging floor-length cylindrical knitted dress, from which garlands of knitted flowers seemed to spring out in a dark and sinister manner. Nature here is powerful and dangerous, threatening and sensual.

Like many independent designers, Volpi 'wanted to see [his] own ideas through to fruition', hence the decision to launch an own label brand. And he has had plenty of paid work, especially teaching, as well as his own studio space. But he has also had to shoulder a lot of responsibility without long-term sponsorship or support of the type provided by the global brands mostly based in Paris and available only to the London fashion 'superstars', and this puts him in a difficult position. After the first two or three years following gradu-ation, it becomes harder and harder to regain the attention of the big sponsors and major companies interested in collaborations. Like our other 'star' designers, Volpi received an initial rush of publicity in the early days, but keeping that up and retaining the attention of the fashion media, from month to month, is hard. Doing undergraduate and graduate work in London gave him extensive professional pathways that included both the possibility of working with well-known Italian companies such as Pitti Filati in Florence, as well as teaching work, while also allowing him to do his own label work. He embodies the overstretched figure of the London designer pushed to pay his bills and keep some sort of cashflow, a situation that can so easily lead to burn-out through sheer overwork, since, with erratic earnings, he can only afford to pay people on an irregular basis. Most recently, and during the pandemic, Volpi has consolidated his teaching role as a lecturer in knitwear, while also beginning to work closely with a sustainable yarn production company based in Hong Kong.

We visited Bruno Basso and Chris Brooke at their South London home in 2015, which at that time they were also using as their studio space. For them, managing to buy a house in the then less expensive neighbourhood of Camberwell was the best way of working as well as living together. They had been in business for nearly a decade and, as prize-winners and with many accolades from *Vogue* magazine as new talent, they had formed collaborations with one well-known Italian producer and with the jewellers Swarovski. Basso and Brooke met as a couple at CSM and produced a prize-winning collection at their degree show with their digital print technique and multicolour textile designs. They were among the first cohort for the Fashion Fringe Award in 2004 and were quickly taken on by the CEO of the Italian brand Aeffe, which offered them an exclusive licensing agreement for the manufacture and distribution of their womenswear. They also got the chance in Italy (with some input also from a Dutch company) to develop a strong knowledge base in advanced digital print techniques. With this new skills base, Bruno trained up his Italian colleagues in this field. Following on from this, Basso and Brooke worked together to develop a very successful own label business model, which won global attention, especially for the menswear, a high colour sport and club aesthetic. Prior to this, most of their work had been in womenswear, designing dresses (including one worn by Michelle Obama). The hallmark of their work has been hi-tech computer-generated patterns that they 'cut-n-mix' onto stretches of fabric to create a collage effect. A shirt may start off plain gold for a few inches down to the chest, then suddenly there is a burst of a vibrant pattern, followed by a thick strip at the bottom of something entirely different. This technique is then followed through in the women's dress collection; for example, the neckline of a dress might move through what looks like three different fabrics, but it is in fact made up of a single strip of silk digitally printed. Over a ten-year period, Basso and Brooke's work was written about extensively in the fashion press, resulting, for example, in the collaboration with Swarovski. The hi-tech digital printing method was in the forefront of new developments across the sector, and, with strong links in Portugal (where they now live), there were opportunities for having the work produced in the various small factory facilities in the Faro region. From womenswear, they shifted into menswear only, and with the move to Portugal they began to step sideways into interiors, including tiles, cushions and, most recently, wallpaper.

The design practice developed by Basso and Brooke demonstrates the way in which the *milieu of labour* has functioned for them in a transnational context at a point in time when globalization was being expressed in a more optimistic vein, as evidenced in these jazzy collections. Their time at CSM resulted in prizes and accolades as well as the chance to develop further their expertise in digital technology. Having got so far with this, they were then able to move to Porto, and to rebuild the business during the pandemic from this cheaper city space. Drawing on their entrepreneurial ingenuity, they paused their fashion work to allow them to concentrate on other design projects, in particular wallpaper. As a professional design pathway, this is not so unusual for graduates from the London art and design schools, and it demonstrates the breadth of practice fostered by the *milieu of labour*. The constantly expanding knowledge base in digital print technology, alongside access to many suppliers as well as the existing collaborative partnerships, frequently leads to widening the range from purely fashion collections into lifestyle and homeware collections.[31]

We now have a wallpaper design company called Jupiter 10. We pioneered the digital print process in the fashion industry in the early to mid-2000s. We had an instantly recognizable aesthetic and quickly established ourselves with the backing of Italian giant Aeffe. To sign a major licensing agreement after showing our first collection of twelve looks was unheard of, and fast-tracked us onto the international fashion circuit. Aeffe produced and licensed collections for Jean Paul Gaultier, Moschino, Alberta Ferretti, Narciso Rodriguez, among others. The business model we work with now is extremely streamlined, one product, one size, one price, many prints. With interior design, particularly with wallpaper, the shelf life is almost limitless, as opposed to fashion where there are at least two main seasons designers work to. I think the transition into this industry has allowed us to focus with time on the longevity of a print, rather than just the relevance of it to that one season, as with fashion. (Email, 18 October 2021)

Basso and Brooke have had to evolve and adapt their studio practice in a fiercely competitive environment. They have stayed loyal to the genres that they started out with and that have become their authorial signatures. London's fashion *milieu of labour* (the art schools) trained them well in this respect, and at a time that was just prior to the rapid escalation of rent, which gave them the foundation for an affordable start to their careers. Since then, the lack of policy for the sector has become more marked.

For me there is a big imbalance in the number of designers … and the lack of industry/governmental business investment opportunities available. It seems there is the constant hunger for new designers but not enough capital to grow and sustain these as viable businesses for the long term. It's a shame when you see so many genuinely gifted designers choosing to bow out, whereas if there were more licensing/production agreements in place to support the growth they could continue to establish. (Email, Chris Brooke, October 2021)

Conclusion

Neoliberal rationality has imposed a 'degradation of labour' in the fashion sector. This mirrors what has happened more widely across the economy, where there has been wage stagnation and where more people than before are working on a freelance, casual or even zero-hours basis. By degradation of labour, we mean the shrinking of the 'talent pool' for all the reasons spelt out so far, especially in cases where low-income students cannot afford the 'tools of the trade'. Endorsement of the winner-takes-all-model leads to the 'precarity of success'. The degradation of labour also applies to the way in which the high-rent economy makes it more difficult for even successful designers to pay their teams higher wages, or to employ more people on a permanent basis. Therefore, what looks like a big success model, as shining new buildings transform the urban landscape, is undergirded by a neoliberal logic that in reality operates to create a city and a fashion sector of social polarization and exclusion. The absence of a strong fashion policy agenda has meant that these issues are overlooked or ignored. Academic teaching staff are also subjects of the neoliberal 'degradation of labour'. They too have seen many years of wage stagnation and increasingly high rates of casualization as well as the proliferation of short-term contracts (McGettigan 2013). The art and design schools are particularly implicated in processes of academic casualization; they have even spearheaded it for the reason that there has long been an ethos of artists, filmmakers and other creative professionals wanting to work part time or on temporary contracts in order to find time for their studio work. This tradition in the art schools has meant that senior managers can all the more easily justify the deteriorating conditions of labour across the workforce. It is only relatively recently that art and design faculty have become more militant and more fully unionized, sometimes taking part in strikes and protests.

For students from outside London, and from low-income working-class families whose 'dream' it may be to study at one of the leading art and design schools, the prospect is now a miserable one, as they are saddled with debt during their undergraduate years, forced to do so many part-time jobs that they cannot give their time and attention to their studies. They then realize that in this field it is further study in the form of an expensive Master's degree that eventually opens doors into the sector. The global university business model confirms London's status as a magnet for 'talent' in the now resurgent creative economy, but this applies to an already privileged cohort only. In the course of this chapter we have addressed two of the more pervasive and pernicious effects – first, that low-income students from working-class and often ethnic minority families, especially those growing up outside London and the South-East, are more excluded than in the past due to the exponential rise in the cost of living and the debt mountain they would need to take on in order to study for a degree in the London schools;[32] and second, the generational cleavage that has emerged, with younger graduates in their twenties and early thirties less visible in the London fashion design scene. Here the degradation of labour means the disappearance of talent and the thinning of the social network. Of course, new names continue to appear in the fashion press each year. Some, like Phoebe English, Bethany Williams, Molly Goddard and Grace Wales Bonner, all major prize-winners, have created their own successful practices, but in a more atomized environment. The established designers who took part in this study and who were willing to give up some time to travel to Glasgow for two days to take part in the CREATe event, or to join the team in Berlin, London and Milan, and to spend time in other daytime and evening events, were all outspoken about the need for better policymaking in fashion and for solutions to be found on questions of studio space, and for the importance of establishing a more socially engaged public image across the sector. In the conclusion of this book, we turn our attention to the need to decentralise fashion practice, and we make a case for puncturing the London bubble and for investing in towns and cities across the UK so that fashion culture can be a source of localized economies and, in the process, can also become more socially diverse.

3

Berlin: Microenterprises and the Social Face of Fashion

The vast quantity of disused spaces available in Berlin – the capital city of one of Europe's largest nations – and the relative freedom and tolerance under which 'temporary uses' were allowed to flourish on such spaces, are rather unusual in comparison with the situation in other European capital cities or large metropolises.

(Colomb 2012)

[In Germany, there has been] a lack of political and social acceptance to classify fashion as a relevant economic and cultural asset.

(Oxford Economics 2021)

Introduction: The precarity of underemployment

The Berlin fashion scene offers a fascinating and ambivalent case for analysis. On the one hand, there is potential for a different kind of fashion practice to emerge that is regional and socially engaged. On the other hand, designers and those in design-related fields, despite the support they receive to get their businesses off the ground, find themselves experiencing the 'precarity of underemployment'. This stems from the historical circumstances of the city's post-Fordist labour market, particularly its repercussions for women in the creative sector. This chapter marks a second and more extended iteration of preliminary research carried out in Berlin between 2012 and 2014 (McRobbie 2016).[1] Many of the labels we observed were female-led fashion start-ups operating primarily at a local level. Their presence as small shops and ateliers dotting street fronts in what were, in 2014, still run-down neighbourhoods brought signs of colour and activity. One respondent, who ran a fashion social enterprise, commented that these signs of feminine creativity had a symbolic effect, one that countered the drab image the neighbourhood had for crime and antisocial activity.[2] While there was inevitably a desire on the part of the designers and store-owners to have the work known about and sold internationally, there was a strong commitment to the city of Berlin itself, and to its distinctive (and vibrant) (sub)cultural life. The dense network of cultural microbusinesses, from start-ups for a huge range of apps, to hostels, boutique hotels and airbnbs for weekend clubbers, from bars and pop-up restaurants, to mega-sized nightclubs and dance venues, and from galleries to expansive studio spaces occupied by some of the world's best-known artists, would inevitably give rise to a home-grown fashion scene. A sprawling subcultural economy has taken root in the city over the years. What was once an informal music and club scene with many offshoots is now consolidated into a set of activities through which the city begins to define itself, such that the 'scene' is a key element of the place-making or city-branding exercises undertaken by the city government (Senate).[3] But at the same time, Berlin has become something of a living laboratory for the playing out of many different political actors and interest groups converging round key issues such as housing, gentrification, the need for rent controls, precarious work and the commercialization of the club scene (Colomb 2012; Lange 2012, 2016; Berfelde 2022).

There has been much discussion of the way in which large companies that rely on a youth culture image poach some of this subcultural capital by setting up stores or HQs in the same areas (such as Mediaspree, Mitte, Kreuzberg), thereby contributing to escalating land values and rent rises (Thornton 1996). These brands (for example, Muji, or the Swedish brand Acne Studio) trade on the overall image of the small-scale designers but with cheaper prices. Unlike in London, the designers gain little from this presence, since the freelance contracts or sponsorships that many London designers can rely on are rare in Berlin. The same is true for fashion-related activities such as photography, styling and set design. This leads to the 'precarity of underemployment'. The store of subcultural capital is reduced and instead is expressed in an insistence on the independent status and non-commercial ethos of the activity. This 'keeping it real' image runs right through many microbusinesses in Berlin in a context where there are few wider economic opportunities. And when things are not going well and customer sales are modest to low, the various actors adopt an understandably defensive tone and take pride in their independence: 'we do the work for its own sake'.[4] There is a dearth of better-paid commercial opportunities for multitasking during slow periods for 'own label work'. This is the context in which small-scale creative workers in Berlin express their opposition and resistance to urban planning, which prioritizes large-scale capital development at the expense of tenants and local business owners. Struggles and activism are defining features of this whole scene, and the Senate recognizes the sector in this contradictory guise, both as part of a growth sector for the city economy and as a force of opposition against further gentrification arising from the presence of finance capital in the housing and property market.

In Berlin, more so than in London and Milan, our participants understood themselves to be very much a part of ongoing political debates about gentrification and about precarious labour in the cultural sector. They were mostly already involved in community and environmental issues, they voiced criticisms about the impact of tourism even when they depended on it for sales. They mostly lived as well as worked in the neighbourhoods where these changes were taking place. Their children went to the local schools. Like many young people, they had first arrived in these areas because there was space to work and affordable rents. A distinctively social and green agenda was inscribed in the various business plans. We develop the idea of social awareness as a defining feature of fashion culture in Berlin throughout the course of this chapter. The Berlin Senate recognizes that many people in the city are working on a freelance or self-employed basis.[5] A raft of policies has been developed, and it is this policy nexus that comprises the Berlin *milieu of labour*. There are programmes for employment training and job creation, there are application processes for subsidized space, and projects for sharing equipment and for access to co-working spaces, and so on. This *milieu of labour* has an explicit social wage function that resonates with modes of social democratic governance, even as they are being transformed into more recognizably neoliberal entities. A social wage historically offsets lower wages for what was traditionally a male industrial workforce. This provided various forms of protection and provision in kind, such as subsidized rent, entitlements, health and welfare benefits, free education for children, playgrounds, libraries, etc. In Berlin, this has been adjusted over the years for the freelance and microbusiness sector, which is noteworthy. But it is a fragile cushion of support. As many commentators have pointed out, Germany has been pursuing welfare reform now for many years, notably with the Hartz IV reforms, which reduced the duration and conditions of unemployment benefit, and which also saw the introduction of so-called mini-jobs (or one-euro-per-day jobs), which in effect have been welfare-to-work initiatives (Standing 2015). These go hand in hand with that other hallmark of the neoliberalization trajectory, namely, wage stagnation. A consistent outcome of these various factors at play in Berlin for creative workers is low take-home pay. Throughout this chapter, we argue that, for the respondents we interviewed in Berlin, there are both some stabilizing mechanisms (social wage) and also a range of destabilizing changes (Hartz IV and welfare reform). They are therefore double subjects of a residual social democratic provision and of individualizing neoliberal rationalities.

Fashion sits in an artist-oriented cultural policy landscape, at the same time as its subjects are pushed towards commercial viability. Its reference points remain local and firmly attached to other adjacent forms of cultural production: the club scene, theatre and performance arts, the circuit of conferences and festivals, the art world and the inflow of international visitors that this city economy brings. This Berlin *milieu of labour* governs partly by means of a social wage (or welfarist undergirding), which is also, as already mentioned, constantly under review and subject to revision. There is also the question of entitlement and who qualifies as a subject of the social wage.[6] The social wage is subject to various terms and conditions; support grants, for example, are time-limited. This produces an atmosphere of anxiety among cultural workers. If rent goes up, the fragile economy, which is based on relatively low take-home pay, is thrown into crisis. Fashion microentrepreneurs are fully tuned into this welfare ecosystem of rent cap, wage stagnation and the need for local government support. We argue here that the active participation of women working in fashion in the city, connected as they are with neighbourhood and community politics, gives rise to a form of female-led 'post-Fordist place-making activity' (Colomb 2012: 138, quoting Stevens and Ambler 2010). The very existence of these microeconomies makes them worthy of study, even as they come up against the market with its unreliable customer base.[7]

Berlin differs from the two other cities in this study in that it is not a centre for global fashion, nor has it had, in the postwar period, a thriving haute couture tradition. There are of course glossy fashion boutiques lined up one after the other and on both sides of the 3.5 kilometre-long old West Berlin boulevard Kurfürstendamm: Dior, Prada, Chanel, Jil Sander, Armani, Dolce e Gabbana and so on. There is the department store KaDeWe. But these are shops, and no world-leading fashion brands have design studios or business headquarters in the city – or indeed in Germany.[8] From the late nineteenth century, and especially during the Weimar Republic, Berlin had a much higher profile; indeed, it was a high fashion centre (Westphal 2020). We need only look at the paintings of the Expressionist period, especially Kirchner's Berlin street scenes, to be reminded of how fashion played an important role in the creation of European urban modernity. The sharp angular boyish looks, the strong eye make-up and dark red lipstick, the bold printed fabrics adopted by young women in the city: this all shows how a femininity that challenged conventional norms came to be part of the urban vista, prompting Simmel's famous essay on fashion (1957 [1904]) and later attracting the attention of Walter Benjamin (1979), whose wife Dora worked for one of the city's fashion magazines. The fashion culture came to exemplify what Simmel labelled the 'blasé attitude' of modern city life. But the key thing here was that this fashion culture, from design through to production and manufacture, was owned and overseen by successful Jewish fashion entrepreneurs, and, as Westphal (2020) documents in detail, by 1933 these companies, mostly located in the Hausvogteiplatz area of the city, were subjected to raids and violent attacks by Nazi thugs and were subsequently violently appropriated and 'Aryanized'. The owners were stripped of their assets, and the entire Jewish personnel were replaced by a non-Jewish and typically inexperienced workforce. Those who could fled to London or New York, while others were, in the coming years, deported and murdered by the Nazis in concentration camps.[9]

Berlin's fashion identity was crushed. Instead, a subdued and conservative Hausfrau-oriented middle market, which (guiltily perhaps) disavowed fashion in favour of serviceable clothing, came to dominate the high streets, exemplified by companies such as Gerry Weber, Baselitz and the younger but equally safe counterpart, Marco Polo.[10] There has never been anything equivalent even to the UK's Marks and Spencer (also originally a Jewish-owned company), known in recent decades for its more upmarket and design-led collections. Nearly eighty years on from the end of the Second World War, this destruction of the fashion industry that took place in Berlin as part of what the Nazis defined as degenerate culture has repercussions for the discussion that follows. The cosmopolitan, outward-looking fashion culture never returned. Instead, since the 1960s, fashion has taken its lead from youth culture and, later, from the 1990s club culture. The absence of a corporate fashion design sector in the city today means that there is a greatly reduced spill-over job market and 'precarity of underemployment'. Underemployment stems from multiple factors. There has always been relatively high unemployment in the city, with a surplus of well-qualified graduate and postgraduate people. The core professions in Berlin, such as teaching in schools, colleges and universities, require rafts of qualifications and they are much more conventionally regulated than is the case in the UK. Nowadays there are more openings, most often in the training and coaching sectors (though these too require certificates and accreditation). There is a lot of competition for part-time teaching contracts, and opportunities for additional earnings to supplement fashion design work are limited. Unlike in London, there are fewer opportunities for independent designers to pick up freelance work with prestigious labels. Nor can they hone their own skills for a few years prior to setting up by working as an assistant for a well-known designer.

The *milieu of labour*: Berlin

The historical absence of a high-fashion identity in Berlin since the 1930s has had two immediately recognizable consequences. First, style and subculture emerged in the late 1960s student movement, giving rise to a hippie alternative economy. In this still walled city, bookstores, bars, hippie and punk hang-outs, gay clubs and second-hand fashion shops all signalled a colourful alternative and radical identity. The impact of feminism throughout this period provided a critique of fashion culture as exploitative of female sexuality, using seductive techniques to create women's reliance on consumer culture. Later, following reunification, various permutations of the non-commercial and alternative street style exploded onto the world stage, as Berlin became the global centre for punk and techno music and its clubs began to generate a night-time economy that, in turn, had a ripple effect across the city, including kick-starting hotels and hostels, budget airlines, bars and restaurants and fashion shops, which were located in streets where this youthful population gathered. The distinctiveness of Berlin's independent fashion scene today more than three decades after reunification inevitably reflects the longevity of this countercultural and self-organized scene.

The second force that has shaped the livelihoods of the designers who took part in this current study is the role of the Berlin local government, the Senate and the various waves of policy decisions developed to help create jobs and improve the economy of the city. As the main *milieu of labour*, the Senate has introduced a wide range of instruments for a population of young people as part of the arts and cultural workforce.[11] The *milieu of labour* is this urban governance apparatus. Tensions emerge for fashion because it is hard for fashion designers to convince policymakers of their 'fine art/conceptual fashion' identities. There is recognition that the fashion design scene is worthy of support, but they are consistently being pushed towards being more commercial.[12] Designers have to create their own 'buzz', often in conjunction with the self-organized activities in the arts, music and start-up tech scenes. The recent *Fashion Council of Germany Report*, somewhat perversely, adhered to the middle ground of the 'clothing sector' only, remarking in passing that there was no equivalent to art and design schools like Central Saint Martins for their capacity to train world-leading designers (Oxford Economics 2021).

The provisions that exist are defined more widely in terms of job-creation initiatives, often taking the form of multi-team projects. These are typically joint-funded initiatives drawing together various agencies including EU social funds as well as local and national organizations. There are also the more standard self-employment schemes.[13] Given that this is the context for fashion start-ups, a 'high fashion' culture is much less visible. There is less snobbishness and more interaction across the different practices of design in the city. These structural factors in the forms of available grants and systems of support provide the undergirding for the microeconomy of fashion. The conditions are that there must be a social inclusion factor, a clear commitment to the environment and to sustainability at every point in the fashion cycle. The fashion social entrepreneurs will also undertake outreach activities with low-income people or with other vulnerable groups with the aim of finding ways of improving their lives. This is a more localized approach to fashion, from design through to production and sales and distribution, supported through various regeneration policies and EU social fund projects that focus on increasing employment levels and creating social cohesion.[14] While fashion design in Berlin invariably looks, sometimes longingly, to the global stage or international catwalk, the reality is that this is a local economy, following its own pathway and focused on its prevailing (but not universal) not-for-profit ethos. The designers we interviewed used local small-scale manufacturers, the furthest just 40 kilometres away over the border into Poland. If we draw these strands together and factor in the leading role of women, what emerges is a socially aware fashion culture that is also underscored by a commitment to environment-friendly processes at all stages.

Fashion creativity in active neighbourhoods

I am doing everything myself. (Stefan Dietzelt)

That you are working 18 hours a day, without making much money, my family are proud ... It is just me, I do everything with two interns and sometimes one freelancer. (Hien Le)

We focused on what had formerly been a poor and neglected residential *Kiez* (neighbourhood), and home to a large population of Turkish-German families. But now there was a growing influx of young, mostly white, Germans as well as a more international cohort of students, artists, musicians, filmmakers and media producers. The cobbled streets in this part of Neukölln are tree-lined and shaded in summer.[15] There are high Berlin Wilhelmine tenements on each side, grand in scale, and with inner courtyards. The recently renovated ones are situated side by side with those badly in need of improvement. Small traditional businesses, from electrical repairs to barbershops, have been joined by organic bakeries, bookstores and fashion ateliers. The single term 'gentrification' does not fully convey the waves of change, especially in a context where young and well-qualified inhabitants, whether longstanding or recent, are the most vocal and organized in their opposition to the encroachment of finance capital and escalating property values. In 2007, for instance, many residential properties lay empty and looking for tenants. Rents were low, hovering around 250 euros a month for a spacious one-bedroom flat. Six years later, the empty flats had filled up mostly with young people in their early twenties drawn from across Europe to Berlin for its club culture in the hope of finding some way of earning a living on the edges of these music scenes, especially in the light of the global 2008 economic and financial crisis. The other areas in which we found ourselves spending time on studio visits, or just looking around the shops, were in Mitte, from Dircksenstrasse to Almstadtstrasse and also Linienstrasse, where the art world tends to gather after hours. Again, this was an affordable area at that time, with a reduced rent for start-ups, though since then the neighbourhood has become a showcase for more upmarket consumer culture and bigger brands, with tourist bars and restaurants nestling alongside shoe stores, hotels and small upmarket designer clothes shops. Finally, we also found ourselves in Kreuzberg in the streets around Kottbusser Tor. This area has a number of small independent fashion shops and it is also a focal point for anti-gentrification campaigning and for the tenant-led organizations that have sprung up in recent years (Berfelde 2022).

The city has struggled with debt and with the high cost of reunification, and it has taken the step, in the face of much local opposition, of selling off valuable land assets mostly for foreign investment. This in turn gives rise to specu-lative property development and the appearance of luxury condominiums right across key locations, for example in the historic Mitte neighbourhood, in Prenzlauer Berg and across Kreuzberg.[16] Fierce battles have been fought over recent years against rent rises and against the takeover on a massive scale by various international finance groups of public housing. There have been dramatic changes over the Berlin skyline, and also on the ground, from street to street, as the sight of new glossy condominiums have appeared in what were previously pleasant, perhaps overgrown, open urban spaces, as if to emulate London's capitulation to finance capital (see Trautvetter 2020; Peter 2021). In early 2021, a new kind of rent control law *(Mietendeckel)* was introduced by the progressive 'Rot-Rot-Grün' (Red-Red-Green) Senate, and many tenants across the city quickly benefited, receiving letters telling them of their new lower monthly rent. A few months later, this ruling was overturned and tenants were asked to return the money they had been given as backdated rent reduction. The existence of a rent cap and the activities of the tenants' associations show that, when faced with concerted opposition and sustained campaigning, local government can be forced to put the brakes on the roller coaster of finance capital and real estate to at least stabilize the housing conditions of existing tenants. Similarly, the Senate was pushed to buy back into public ownership some areas of real estate that had been bought by the company Deutsche Wohnen and Co., a company that owns more than 130,000 properties in Berlin (Sullivan 2021). Various commentators have pointed to the huge legal hurdles that would need to be overcome for this to happen. More realistically, there will be pressure on landlords to abide by a new rent cap.

These battles to preserve existing social housing provision and to resist the encroachment by predatory forces representing the array of global finance companies connect with our focus on fashion microenterprises because what is at stake is the social wage that de facto allows their activities to carry on, especially during tough times. If rents rise and the studio spaces disappear to be replaced by luxury condominiums, the foundations of working life crumble. From securing affordable space, to getting access to programmes of support and mentorship, our respondents all cited the various projects and programmes.[17] The *milieu of labour*, as the assemblage of urban cultural policymaking activities, impinges on the day-to-day realities of the creative workers. There are worries about its provisions (for example, the rent cap, or a grant for equipment) being reduced in scale or removed altogether. Its defining presence over the livelihoods in the city makes the *milieu of labour* an instrument of the 'risk society', a system for the governance of abnormal work (Beck 2000).

The urban political economy regarding the creative sector is defined through this range of programmes and interventions. Ostensibly designated for training, upskilling and to extend the net of vocational education, and thus directed towards a less well-qualified cohort, the schemes, particularly those funded by the EU, in fact bring together a wide range of academics and postdoctoral students, as well as designers and small-scale producers, including knitters, seamstresses, pattern cutters, etc. The terms and conditions of these grants mean that the designers find themselves organizing their design activity and their livelihoods in conjunction with the constant round of applying for grants. There is from the start a more sociological conversation taking place than would ever be the case in London because the designers are working on these neighbourhood projects with economic geographers and social scientists. At the same time, everyone is aware of the shortcomings of the provisions. Many designers report that the grants for subsidized rent for studio and shop space do not last long enough. One of the prize-winning designers we interviewed, Hien Le, insisted that it takes more than seven years to get established. Another respondent, Esther Perbandt, reiterated this point, after fifteen years of independent working in the city. The designers constantly refer to the recent rises in rents across neighbourhoods that, in the past, were affordable (see Kalandides 2014). Despite the protections, tenants still find themselves under pressure to move out to make way for businesses more able to pay higher rents. These issues are subject to heated debate across the sector in ways that break down barriers between those apparently more successful and those just managing to keep their enterprises afloat. The precarity of underemployment means there is a flattening effect and, in the absence of a high-end haute couture presence, this creates a sense of equality and solidarity.

During the period of research, the *Zwischennutzung* system for the temporary use, at very low rent, of empty property, was run by the devolved neighbourhood companies Quartiersmanagement (QM). At the time of writing, these local offices continue to provide working space to applicants depending on availability and on the social value to be delivered by the creative project. For the designers we interviewed in the period from 2013 to 2017, it was possible, through the QM offices, to apply to landlords whose buildings were currently empty. These possibilities for good-quality space had a positive effect, making the idea of setting up in business without any substantial (or very little) financial backing a realistic option. Unlike in London, there is no requirement to be a prize-winner. The idea of gaining access to almost free space is beyond the wildest dreams of London designers. One respondent, Stefan Dietzelt, said that to begin with he had the use of a studio space and shop for free; another mentioned that she was 'really happy right now because I still have a good renting contract'. These schemes for finding a space were relied on by designers and fashion producers. They made a working life possible. Many stitchers, knitters, designers, crafters and makers were based in the Neukölln neighbourhood where, as mentioned above, a number of properties had been lying empty. As we have described elsewhere, designers embellish the shop/studio/salon space to create their brand image (McRobbie 2016). Some, like Nadelwald, Rita in Palma and NEMONA, embrace a slightly ironic aesthetic of crumbling elegance and grandeur. Their high-ceilinged chandeliered spaces are typically furnished to create the ambience of a French haute couture atelier, but with second-hand or up-cycled pieces. Antique chairs, vintage coffee tables and evidence of a flurry of activity can be seen in the background, where there are machinery and equipment as well as bales of fabric and balls of wool for knitting. The visibility of the work process is a feature of this female-led 'post-Fordist place-making activity' (Colomb 2012: 138, quoting Stevens and Ambler 2010).[18] There is, in these styles of interior décor, a careful interweaving of place and neighbourhood, since the activity typically opens out to the street. The persona of the designer and the creative dynamics of her own working practice are clearly on display. The city is not just a backdrop, but also a raison d'être for working in this kind of way. Designers and salon managers take time to show visitors around their premises.[19]

Social fashion in the city

There are three different forms of fashion practice in the city: the art school-trained avant-garde designers, the social fashion entrepreneurs and the more dispersed and less visible individual homeworkers who are knitting and sewing to make ends meet (Kalandides 2014). Michael Sontag exemplifies the aspirational high-end designer image. He has become a well-known name in the German fashion media for his sculptured bias-cut silk womenswear collections. He has been supported by the Senate to take part in the Berlin showroom in Paris and New York. He comes closest to the *auteur* image of the fashion designer. As he commented in one of our discussions:

On the one hand, I would love to be able to find an agent so that I could show my work in London. An ideal space would be something like the Dover Street Market. On the other hand, I live and work here in Berlin, it is my city and I cannot think how I could move to London. The agents and the buyers do not really look seriously in Berlin, and even with the showroom system set up by the Senate for New York, London and Paris, it has not really benefited the Berlin designers. (Interview, June 2014)

We followed Sontag as he took a number of decisions based on the kind of identity he had already established as a prize-winning German designer. He acquired his own small shop in Kreuzberg and he was able to rely on a flow of interns to help him on a range of tasks. Because of the good press coverage and his overall visibility, he had a number of contracts to work with a couple of German shoe brands, which brought in an income but did not have the leverage of high-end UK collaborations. Within two years of opening the shop Sontag decided that he wanted to move away from the pressure of seasonal shows and annual collections.

I became more aware of the wastage of unsold stock accumulating in the shop when items had to be made up in many different sizes. My costing puts the pieces out of reach for middle range income customers, but this is also because I pay the production team fair wages. So I have opted for a bespoke or on-demand only business model, showing just a limited collection seasonally and taking direct orders. This means that I'm not overproducing. I work like an artist and that's my training. From the start I was not really able to think commercially [laughs]. It was beyond me. The thing about Berlin is that I am able to think through what it is I am doing, the slower pace allows this.[20] (Interview, June 2016)

Other well-known independent designers struggled with the problem of not having enough customers and, like Sontag, they become adept at devising ways of managing solutions to this situation. Esther Perbandt, as we will see below, has partnered with theatre professionals and musicians to bring her work into these performance spaces. In coming up with such ideas, designers also develop a better understanding of the arts and cultural policy regime.[21] They need tourists who are tuned in to the distinctive Berlin styles and the anti-glamour aesthetic, and this means they need the Senate to promote the city in the right way. They can also find customers from within the art crowd. Their shops and studios (typically combined into one atelier-style space) are to be found on busy streets in the areas we have described as active neighbourhoods. These are places flagged up in the weekly 'what's on' newsletters as interesting shopping locations. At weekends, they are places where locals and tourists mingle. And of course, the possibility to be able to have workspaces like these hinges on the various schemes aimed at reducing rents, as well as grants for equipment and so on. If we also factor in the existence of a health insurance scheme for arts and cultural workers,[22] designed to be affordable for freelance modest earners, and alongside this the rent controls in place for domestic properties, we could argue that the 'social' model of fashion that emerges is the product of the *milieu of labour* that facilitates a social wage for the freelance and self-employed sector. This comprises some support for everyday social reproduction – i.e., rent cap, unemployment benefits, affordable childcare in the form of the *Kita*, reliable healthcare and so on.[23] A social wage makes the freelance sector of Berlin fashion designers viable. Historically, the social wage was predicated on the mainstream employment patterns of industrial society and the male breadwinner. But in times of post-Fordism and with the increasing presence of women in the workforce, this patriarchal social contract that emerged in the advanced economies of the postwar period has been adjusted to take women into account as economic agents. The social wage replaces what was previously referred to as the family wage. The *milieu of labour* here is a localized example of the management of precarity and underemployment. It is an assemblage of state facilities stretching from the high-level and longstanding policies that relate to work, employment and self-employment, all the way down to fine-tuned instruments and projects for training and vocational education. The result is a sector of creatives whose take-home earnings do not rise significantly, and for whom there are ups and downs but who usually manage to find ways of keeping afloat. In Berlin, if they do close shop, other opportunities arise, perhaps after some short period of unemployment. Unemployment, because it is viewed as being short term, does not carry any stigma, nor do recipients of benefits feel ashamed, as they have been made to do so in the UK. Instead, there is a common-sense approach. The social wage plays this role of protecting the population; it keeps more highly qualified people in work or in projects that provide bridges into work. It chimes well with what Ulrich Beck (2000) referred to as new modes of underemployment fitted to the postindustrial society of the West.

Fashion as art, fashion as social enterprise

In this section we take the work of designers to explore the themes so far outlined in the chapter and to advance the argument about the *milieu of labour* as a governmental assemblage incorporating a social wage element. The term social enterprise has a different inflection from its meaning in the UK. As Emma Dowling (2020) points out, the idea of social enterprise was, in recent years, the product of the David Cameron Conservative government's promotion of the 'Big Society'. Cameron wanted to advocate a community volunteer spirit, combined with a small business (or one-person company) take-over of various local social services. In the UK fashion sector, the term is used loosely to indicate a system of support given to young designers to develop their business acumen. It simply means being in receipt of some mentoring or other support, with no particular obligation to demonstrate social value. In Germany, the term social enterprise has also gone through various incarnations, most recently referring to the idea of the social business model, but for our purposes here the term applies most directly to the not-for-profit sector.[24] These are local initiatives, sometimes taking place, at least in the early stages, under a bigger umbrella such as an EU social fund project. Marte Hentschel exemplifies the social entrepreneur scene in Berlin. She trained originally in fashion design and then moved into producer services (Common-works) on a not-for-profit basis. This meant partnering Berlin designers with the best and most local small-scale manufacturers. Since 2016, this model has undergone further shifts due to the huge growth in digital services and e-commerce. First, Hentschel moved the producer services to a fully online model, while also expanding the network thanks to a grant from the EU. Sourcebook then became Sqetch, which was an even larger platform, providing a range of services for sustainable production and for ethical practices in supply chain labour.[25] The focus now is on creating a digital platform for producer services informed by a green and social justice agenda. The company has also branched out to provide training and upskilling events and short courses.

Fashion designers need to be tuned into what is going on in the Senate cultural department and about upcoming urban planning issues. Many said they would be pleased to have sponsorship from some of the big brands, so it is not as if there is a purely anti-commercial ethos. The strength of the fashion sector depends on how successfully it pursues an environmental strategy of sustainability. This, along with local outreach work, is where the public good was being served by the small-scale fashion sector. It was the unifying theme across the sector, which extended to vintage shops and up-cycling stores. Environmentalism and the not-for-profit status provided the rationale for the social enterprise ethos. The greening of fashion, the encouragement of local manufacturing, the foregrounding of traditional skills such as knitting, sewing and crocheting, the endorsement of a 'crafts' ethos, and the harnessing of social media and new technology for all of these purposes, provided the underpinning for many of the activities. Alongside this was the emphasis on encouraging women's employment, supporting low-skilled women to improve their qualifications, helping migrant and refugee women to become economically active and providing mentorship and work experience for under-achieving girls in local schools. During the course of our work, we encountered four social enterprises, one of which (Rita in Palma) we document in more detail below. The others were NEMONA, Common-works and Nadelwald (which sadly no longer exists).

> I started off as a medical student but quickly found it was not for me. I had always been interested in fashion and it took me a bit of time to settle on the kind of studio I wanted to

have. To begin with when I found the premises in Neukölln, my father helped me with funds to get started, and when that ended I went to one of the ethical banks and qualified for some support there. The business model then grew quickly as I could see the value of specializing in upmarket fashion accessories and as I realized that there were many women in the neighbourhood, at that point mostly Turkish-German, who had crochet skills and who also could work for me in a safe environment and also earn money where otherwise they were at home. Over the years I have built a bigger team and many of the women come from countries across the Middle East from Lebanon and from Iran. (Cartensen interview, July 2016)

We met with Ann-Kathrin Carstensen, owner of the Rita in Palma label, several times over the period of our research. She enthusiastically took part in lengthy discussions held in her Neukölln atelier, and we also invited her to join our trip to Glasgow in Scotland – though pregnancy meant she was unable to do so. Like several others in our cohort, Carstensen is a mother of young children, and her business model as a social and cultural entrepreneur is organized so that she can work hours that fit in with childcare. Her label has become a well-known presence in the city. She produces a luxury-craft range of accessories, including crochet collar-style neck-pieces designed to be worn with an evening dress, 1940s retro-style crocheted socks, hairpins, burlesque 'bra tassles', bracelets that combine crochet work with stones and crystals, earrings that share the same intricate lacework in combination with stones, and other items of floral- or nature-derived jewellery, as well as 'unique bridal couture'. Most of the items, from the 'bee necklaces' to the chokers, are made in the same palette, from watery pinks to blues and purples and from faded greys to black.[26] As a social entrepreneur in this not-for-profit business, Carstensen oversees everything from the social and community aspects of the work, for example 'crochet evenings', to the more press-oriented activities. This is a niche social enterprise model. Carstensen has attracted a lot of media attention, and, because hers is an accessory business, she does not have the high costs of putting on runway shows. In 2018 she expanded online sales and, at the same time, her work was stocked by fourteen boutiques in Germany and

Switzerland. Alongside this, she was offered a pop-up area in the luxury department store KaDeWe. During the pandemic crisis of 2020–1, Carstensen quickly moved to having her team produce high-quality washable silky-cotton face masks, available for sale online.

The women who crochet, and who make the jewellery, hear about the studio either by word of mouth or from local job centres. Like other social enterprises in the city, Carstensen connects with the job centres with the aim of gaining accreditation for the training and the work experience she provides. She also works closely with community associations in the Neukölln neighbourhood. She said that she was learning Turkish so as to feel closer to her team. She also set up an associated enterprise to help Turkish women learn German (Rita's Haekel Club EV, renamed von Meisterhand in 2019[27]). The studio space becomes a lively place of conversation, activity and social events. Carstensen is able to make use of the Berlin *milieu of labour* as it endorses a social cohesion model of integration for migrant populations. In this case, the model is adjusted as a 'gender mainstreaming' project to empower and support migrant women. But it is also more than this. The element of female-led 'post-Fordist place-making' means foregrounding community, pleasure and women's friendship as a counter to racial hostility. Sociologically speaking, we could ask many more questions about this kind of initiative. Where are the voices of the women crocheters themselves, for example? And what chances do they have to set up their own similar social enterprise? In the multicultural women's community project, the Muslim women work seated next to each other around a large table that is positioned prominently so that customers and visitors can see what they are doing. On the one hand, this is meant to give pride of place to their work; on the other, it can easily feel a little staged.

Their work is carefully curated and displayed in the shop window and in glass boxes mounted along the walls inside the studio. The fashion niche that the label has created relies on a hyperfeminine aesthetic, delicate lingerie pieces and crochet accessories with jewellery, and hybrid pieces that range from craft to high-end couture. There is a dreamy, romantic, sensual quality in all the pieces of work on display, and in the visual images found on the website. Female desire, sexuality and women's pleasures are invoked, as if to overcome divisions of ethnicity and religion and to suggest a realm of freedom and independence.[28] The whole project fits well within the German and, more widely, the EU-supported, gender mainstreaming ethos. Similar projects have sprung up in Berlin and elsewhere in Germany with the arrival of refugees from Syria. More mundane than Rita in Palma, these other projects are usually phrased in terms of preserving traditional skills and crafts such as kilim- and rug-making. There are doubtless many questions that radical voices in the Turkish-German feminist community will surely ask. We could easily envisage further unfoldings of social and cultural entrepreneurship being undertaken by the migrant women sewers and crocheters themselves. Meanwhile, the work opens up and sustains a conversation between women across divides of ethnicity about love, sex, beauty, sensuality and desire.

The work of Esther Perbandt stands in sharp contrast to Rita in Palma's dreamy retro-femininity. At a glance, Perbandt conveys, in her own personal style, the template for her various collections. She is tall and thin and pale, she wears only black or grey, typically with an exaggerated elongated peaked cap, which she teams with layers of punk jewellery, chains and studs. She wears stacked high black wedges with a pom-pom, teamed with her own grey-black angular shirts, asymmetrical skirts or trousers. This image, with gestures to goth, punk and sex club styles, while also being tuned into the tastes of older customers of all genders working in the arts and cultural fields, makes her a striking figure who is often featured in the fashion and music diary sections of the local press. She oversees her own social media presence and she posts on Facebook her travels, the events she takes part in, the shows and the after-show parties. She also documents everything from family gatherings to her experience on a popular German TV show, where she was invited to compete to be Germany's Next Top Designer, and then, even more prominently, on the TV designer competition *In the Cut*. On Instagram and Twitter, she uploads information about new shoots, new collections, new activities. She works collaboratively with artists and musicians. Not long ago, she designed a collection for classical musicians to wear while performing with the orchestra, thus breaking the conventional formal evening wear dress codes with her deep rich colours. She also did a project with a choir, and, on another occasion, for Berlin fashion week, she partook in a runway show, singing as a 'rockstar', with images of the clothes from the collection shown on a backscreen. Her non-traditional wedding collection attracted a lot of media attention in *German Vogue*. Overall, the Esther Perbandt label draws on the historical resources of the city and stages them as part of the work. In this way, she establishes and extends a fashion relation with streets, buildings, cinema history, theatre history and the subcultural repertoire of the Berlin archive. Her pieces express a rock music/rock star aesthetic, dark, masculine, dramatic. In one runway collection, she presented the very elderly Brecht Ensemble actor Valeska Gert (who also appeared in the Berlin avant-garde films of Ulrike Ottinger). At the other end of the spectrum, she joined a film crew to make a documentary about textile production in Bangladesh, which drew attention to exploitation and environmental dangers running through the supply chains in fashion production. More recently, her work was displayed in a Hamburg art gallery.[29]

Perbandt's work is angular, tailored, layered, often asymmetrical, entirely ungendered, sometimes with pin stripes, and in its uses of black, grey, charcoal and a splash of white, it is painterly as well as architectural. The Esther Perbandt shop on Almstadtstrasse in Mitte also serves as a social centre for events that she hosts to attract customers. She too, like Michael Sontag, provides a personal customized service and does her best to attract people into the shop with an after-hours 'private friends shopping experience'.[30]

How do Perbandt's pieces, her collections, shows and the items on the rails in her shop, 'speak' to her audiences, her customers, to the window shoppers and browsers of her Facebook and Instagram pages? What is the life of these objects? Perbandt's fashion emphasizes a 'pop kultur' lineage, but they are not 'pop' in the fast fashion sense. Nor are they simply clubwear for hot sweaty spaces. Although influenced by pop, they are theatrical pieces for the street, for events and for parties. She has created a kind of dramatic David

Bowie look (her background includes mime and performance arts). By staging her work as multimedia pieces in many different locations across the city (also taking it to Paris, Los Angeles and New York), Perbandt makes a loud claim for Berlin fashion. She insists on its importance, in her own case as a style that speaks of tensions, of gender fluidity, of history and of refusals of conventional femininity. There is a dialogue with the city itself, its cultural history, and there is a frustration and an undercurrent of anger that, as an art form, fashion still has to fight for its place. Perbandt mixes three elements in her work: the subcultural, the motif of Berlin itself, and the fine art conceptual dynamic. The *milieu of labour* we have described provides an underpinning to the extent that her performance art brings her closer to the subsidized high art sector, while rent controls allow her to remain in one of the busiest streets in the Mitte neighbourhood, close to galleries, bars and restaurants, and the rent on her own living accommodation is reduced on the grounds that she performs some caretaking activities for the block – and has done so for many years.

Perbandt's work consistently registers the subcultural identity of the Berlin club scene, which from the 1990s has become a world-renowned phenomenon, and a valuable economic asset. Her collections move away from the low-key style of the dance scene in favour of a dark goth and rock music aesthetic. While club culture fashion in London is a key feature of many catwalk shows (from Alexander McQueen's bumster trousers to Pam Hogg's silky catsuits), this kind of articulation of pop culture is less frequent in Germany. As Manske (2021) has argued, fashion studies were for many years located entirely in the lower status technical grade of high school and then in further education. Fashion has had to fight to be taken seriously in the long-established art and design schools, disavowing both the commercial cycles of the mid-market fashion scene, as well as the imbrication of fashion in pop music culture. This resulted in a shrunken fine art fashion practice in undergraduate and Master's programmes, at least up until the 2010s. It would require a thorough sociological review of what this kind of fashion pedagogy in Germany comprises to substantiate our comments here. In the absence of such research, we can at least draw attention to various factors: (a) the recent flowering of private fashion design schools and universities, suggesting that these are popular subjects for young people; (b) the, perhaps strategic, emphasis in this provision on business, management and marketing; (c) the muted presence of a pop aesthetic in fashion pedagogy in the main art and design universities; and (d) the absence of a required cultural studies component in the art and design curriculum, which, in the UK, theorizes and validates the idea of subculture and of youth culture as historically significant phenomena. In the more liberal, indeed radical, educational context of the UK secondary school system, GCSE and A-level fashion and textile studies are highly regarded subjects on the curriculum, part of what goes on in the art departments up and down the country. These are the challenges with which someone like Perbandt is confronted. If the dance and DJ scene remains a male-dominated field, then it would take a feminist cultural studies approach to untangle the gender dynamics and the hoops she has to climb through in order to position her work boldly and unapologetically between the art world and club culture.[31]

Conclusion

In Germany, fashion still has to fight against its frivolous, feminine and non-feminist status. Its assumed place in the mainstream of consumer culture suggests that feminist academic and political battles that have been fought and won in the UK and in the English-speaking world have had less resonance in German cultural life and in the academy (Manske 2021). In the academic left we can attribute this to the dominating influence of critical theory and the Frankfurt School. In this context the post-2000 creative economy discourse steps forward and offers an alternative legitimizing framework. The urban cultural policy terrain is the *milieu of labour*. Perbandt stands out for her spirited insistence on the aesthetics of punk and post-punk rock music (the Bowie image) to make her case for the importance of fashion. Meanwhile, the Oxford Economics report on the status of German fashion (2021) bemoans the absence of powerhouse art schools like CSM in London, and adds that Germany loses its talent to these British institutions, but without suggesting that fashion should be more visible on the school curriculum in Germany. These factors all have an adverse effect on the fashion scene in Berlin, meaning that it is reliant on club culture and on the activities that have grown up around this dance and techno economy. This, alongside Senate initiatives to support local cultural enterprises, is where fashion is located. The hard work of establishing a fashion presence has been mostly undertaken by a female cohort of designers and shop owners who have forged a path for a fashion culture to thrive. In a context where there is not a sizeable customer base for many of the pricey items, and where small micro-enterprises struggle to survive, with designers and shop owners themselves earning only modest salaries over the years, those in the fashion industry are very much part of the precarious cultural workforce. The *milieu of labour* (as a social wage) both manages and oversees this self-organized world of female-led 'abnormal work' (Beck 2000). The precarity of underemployment referred to throughout this chapter reflects the double process of subjectivation for this workforce. Over the decades, high unemployment in the city, even for its well-qualified inhabitants, has encouraged self-employment and, in our context, fashion microenterprises. The state supports these endeavours that are informed simultaneously by a neoliberal rationality that understands how hard young people will work to realize a self-expressive project, and also by a residual, maybe reluctant, social democratic ethos in the form of the social wage and its welfarist underpinnings. This combination has produced a social field that is uncertain, but that also has potential for the future of creative work. All the people we have foregrounded in this chapter have shown that fashion can be done on a different kind of basis, and according to a different rhythm; it can be more embedded in local, regional communities without having to take the lead from Paris, London, Milan or New York. And this can happen without relinquishing a fine art ethos, a commitment to imagination, fantasy and style. With public investment, a community economy of ethical and sustainable fashion practice becomes possible. And this is a model that could be rolled out in many other cities, such as Glasgow, Montreal, Portland (Oregon), Detroit, São Paolo, Johannesburg, Kingston (Jamaica), thereby puncturing the power of the global brands and creating a viable alternative.

4

Milan: Fashion Microenterprises and Female-led Artisanship

'Made in Italy' romanticizes small craft-based firms competing against the odds on the unforgiving field of hardscrabble capitalism.

(Ross 2004: 212)

[Milan is] the most active hub of global and local flows of design innovation ... a complex and extended mega-region ... where the boundaries between metropolitan and non-metropolitan spaces tend to disappear.

(Bertacchini and Borrione 2010: 146)

A characteristic of Milanese fashion is its development in relation to the industrial system.

(Vanni 2016: 443)

And at parties at least we can say truthfully that we are designers.

(Interview with Flatwig Milan)

Introduction: City of global brands

In this chapter we identify a key factor that accounts for the very different status of fashion microenterprises in Milan compared to the other cities in this study. Because fashion has long counted as a major industry, with activities spread across the country, albeit more concentrated in the north, there appears to be no sociopolitical rationale for including it in the more emergent creative economy, which, up until very recently, has had only a fledgling status in the field of urban and regional policymaking. We might also assume that fashion's feminine image accounts for its historically being taken less seriously by government than other equivalent enterprises – for example, the car industry. In this context, and in the light of exceptionally high graduate unemployment following the financial crisis of 2008, we locate the informal and independent fashion economies that have sprung up in the Milan area as (a) related both directly and indirectly to the radical campaigns and new waves of left-wing activism by young people in the city from 2005 onwards; (b) a phenomenon that fills the gap left by the remains of the Third Italy and its post-Fordist regional model of fashion districts; and (c) as activities nowadays led by young women determined to be active in the labour market and able to tap into a historical *milieu of labour* provided by family tradition and heritage models from the artisanal workshops now adapted to become fashion studio spaces. We also note a historical irony whereby the Third Italy model found its way to the UK as a neo-Marxist strategy for innovation in the late 1980s, which in turn paved the way for the New Labour government of 1997 championing the 'talent-led economy' and the culture industries.

Milan is our third case study for investigating fashion microenterprises. The city is of course known for the central role it plays in hosting seasonal collections and for being home to many global luxury fashion brands (Breward and Gilbert 2006). While Rome remains the national centre for the film industry and for public broadcasting, Milan, especially since the time of Silvio Berlusconi's leadership, became home to a range of new small radio and TV stations as well as newspapers and fashion magazines. Fashion is, in effect, built into the architecture of the city, from the welcoming Armani signage and the array of billboards that greet visitors as they arrive at its airports, to its equally visually adorned main thoroughfares, as if the well-known brands direct the traffic, providing an itinerary for a fashion-aware population, as well as for visitors; from landmarks like the Armani Hotel on the main shopping avenue, Via Alessandro Manzoni, to award-winning buildings like the Prada HQ on the Via Antonio Fogazzaro. The result of carefully planned urban brand strategies, contemporary luxury fashion is boldly and confidently inserted, as if to claim a rightful place for itself alongside the historic buildings, the churches, the Cathedral and the ancient city walls. This is not an obtrusive commercial presence, but rather a key element of national culture. The advertisements and billboards, for bags, shirts, shoes, tights and many other fashion items, suggest a rhetoric of belonging; the Italian tradition of artisanship is at the heart of the culture and the economy, a 'homage to craft antiquity' (Ross 2004: 210). The image is one of high-end or luxury 'designer-led' fashion made from fine fabrics and created by a workforce whose skills have been honed and passed down over the centuries. In this context, the idea of start-up culture and, indeed, of independent design-led small-scale fashion enterprises does not spring to mind when considering the fashion identity of the city.

The mainstream culture is corporate, luxury and glossy. And while Milan and its immediate environment have been designated as a 'magical circle' for the dense concentration of fashion and textile-related activity, this in itself does not necessarily lead to the kinds of informal 'indie' fashion microenterprises that have such a distinctive visibility in both London and Berlin (Dunford 2006; Bertacchini and Borrione 2010). Even with a more progressive municipal council in place in Milan since 2012, most accounts of creative economy activity refer to a 'lack of institutional support' and 'scant investment' (see, e.g., D'Ovidio and Cossu 2017). Paolo Volonte comments that 'all the main Milanese fashion schools maintain close contacts with industry' (2012: 430). However, despite the high status of the Domus Academy and the Politecnico, these relations with the industry do not seem as highly charged and as widely publicized as they are in the UK. Nor do we find the city council or the national government working to provide an apparatus of support in the form of employment projects or access to subsidized space and equipment for young creatives, as has been the case in Berlin. Instead, as we found, one key incentive for getting involved in a fashion start-up stemmed from the superfluous population of arts, media and fashion graduates and workers in the city and the high rate of unemployment or semi-employment, as well as the psychological stress in the wake of the financial crisis of 2008. There was also frustration with the mainstream fashion houses for operating in opaque ways regarding recruitment.[1]

The fashion activity we encountered overlapped with waves of left-wing activism in the Milan area, including groups of software and tech activists who, in the early 2000s, took over abandoned space in the city and organized new kinds of sharing and collaborative economies, including the setting up of 'fab labs' that aimed at showing that it was possible to imagine an alternative way of doing fashion (Fantone 2007; Raunig 2013; Romano 2018).[2] Ilaria Vanni (2016) provides a lucid account of the first wave in 2005 of anti-precarity activism in the field of fashion in Milan. As it transpires, three figures who played key roles in this Situationist-style hijacking of Milan Fashion Week, with the staging of a catwalk show by an invented and non-existent designer whom they named 'Serpico Naro', joined our CREATe team as consultants and advisers.[3] This intervention and the publicity that followed drew attention to the exploitation and precarious working conditions on the edges of the industry in the Milan region. The fashion items themselves epitomized a critique of the idealization of bodily norms and the mythologizing ideology of *auteur* creativity (Vanni 2016). Giannino Malossi (2002), a leading labour organizer, looked to Marx's *Grundrisse* and to the idea that machine technology could potentially free up the workforce, giving them more time to discuss their working conditions and possibly become more militant (the 'general intellect'). The more recent age of cognitive capitalism furthers this potential, while also giving rise to economic activities that came to be known as 'immaterial labour' (Lazzarato 1996). The new forms of collectivity based on 'free labour' also provide a framework for 'autonomous forms of urban effervescence' (Terranova 2004; Arvidsson et al. 2011).[4] As the industry is transformed, and especially with the growth of digital and social media, the workforce finds itself with access to a range of tools that it can 'divert' to its own radical purposes. This was borne out in the subsequent 'fab lab' actions led by Zoe Romano in Milan, who championed an idea of a 'WeMake' DIY fashion system through opensource patterns and self-creations. (In the empirical section below, we draw attention again to the 'fab-lab' activities at the Isola space in Milan.)

Following up on these new forms of anti-precarity activism in 2004, in 2012 hundreds of young people took over a skyscraper building owned by the wealthy Ligresti family. As Marianna D'Ovidio and Alberto Cossu describe, the occupation was organized by graduates in arts and cultural fields ('knowledge and cultural workers') who were challenging the conditions of precarity they were faced with, as well as the failure on the part of both national government and the municipality of Milan to engage with the severity of these circumstances (D'Ovidio and Cossu 2017; Cossu 2022). This movement became known as Macao – an independent centre for art, culture and research. There was wide public support for the activists, and the newly elected left-wing municipality was prepared to listen, such that, over time, Macao has come to represent a force for negotiation on various issues of urban cultural politics. The events supported by the organization, including art exhibitions and theatre performances, were all underpinned by ideas of social justice and economic redistribution and, as D'Ovidio and Cossu emphasize, by politics shared with other European arts-led precarity activism, focusing on 'bottom-up' organization, including making the case for the right to housing. The fashion start-ups that figured in our CREATe study (2013–17) by and large did not see themselves as being part of a bigger social project. The protagonists did not cohere as a group. What they mostly shared in common was that setting up a fashion microenterprise and being self-employed was a source of psychological relief, and an escape from the loss of identity that came with being economically inactive, or with being threatened by redundancy or being entirely dependent on family. And, as we will show, gender is an important factor here, to the extent that young women can also be seen to be taking over and replacing the kinds of artisanship that, in the past, were exclusively male activities and that were now seen as declining as this workforce aged.

Various reports mention that for some time there had been a generational flight away from the kind of artisanal work that young people associated with their parents and the long hours they had to put in to make ends meet, and that a gradual reversal of this flight, led by young women, was now in evidence (Hadjimichalis 2006). Apart from Carolina Bandinelli's 2019 book, little has been written about the wider context of social enterprise activity, start-ups and the co-working economy in Milan and, more widely, in Italy as a whole. In Milan, we saw no sign of small-scale fashion scenes in the city streets. What was visible was the broad sweep of family-owned fashion boutiques and small-scale retailers that line the streets of almost every Italian town. (Unfortunately, we cannot be sure about how these small independently owned shops provide outlets for young aspiring designers to sell their work. We could surmise that, with local or family connections, this is a way of getting bags, or dresses, or scarves and other items into the shop windows.)

The documents and reports that appear under the rubric of creative economy in Italy, and that seek to bridge a gap between the relevant sectors, have a strongly regional approach rather than a focus on individual cities like Milan, Florence or Rome (Pisoni 2012; Unioncamere/Symbola 2013). And moves to establish initiatives for developing a national creative economy strategy have tended to omit fashion design (Albanese et al. 2014). This is because fashion is already understood as a key industry and manufacturing sector and therefore not part of the cultural and art world. It is only relatively recently that universities have provided formal training in fashion design.[5] This makes sense if we acknowledge the central place occupied by fashion in Italy's mainstream economy. Fashion is a major industrial player, with its own annual calendar of events and attendant publicity. It is more like the car industry, and has been almost wholly male-dominated until recently, operating something of a closed shop.[6] As a leading industry, it has, however, never been in the political spotlight; it never experienced the waves of strikes and occupations that the car industry experienced in the 1970s, nor did it become the focal point for sociological research and Marxist theory, as happened in the collaborations between factory workers and university militants in that period. Only the *détournement* anti-precarity events of 2005 changed this picture (Vanni 2016). Instead, the more widely dispersed manufacturing bases across Italy for fashion and clothing have included large and small factories, originally with a skilled male workforce at the core of activities and otherwise relying on countless numbers of homeworkers – mostly women on piece rates and doing finishing work on small items such as gloves or woollen accessories (Steele 2003). Since the late 1990s, this division of labour has been shaken up and replaced, after periods of off-shoring by the big companies, with re-shoring activities, including small shop-based manufacturing, springing up in towns like Prato and drawing on low-paid immigrant labour. Here the hierarchies, including the owners, the middlemen and the supply chains, are even more opaque, with the rise of many Chinese-Italian fashion production entrepreneurs (Max 2018).

A parallel artisanal workshop system has existed alongside this, usually specializing in leather goods or else working with silks and other fine textiles, and these too have been male-dominated small businesses into which only very recently have women dared to enter. Sometimes both an artisanal workshop system and a small manufacturing base are to be found together, for example in the Perugian town of Solomeo, where a large percentage of the entire population is employed by Brunello Cucinello to produce the famous cashmere jumpers ('sporty chic') and other menswear items loved by US golfers and CEOs in their leisure time, and stocked in exclusive boutiques across the world (Mead 2010). Given the complexity of the entire fashion industrial system in Italy, our own investigations have had to be reconfigured as we consider the case of Milan. Independent fashion seems to exist as a kind of shadow fashion economy, without the formal recognition of being a key part of the new urban creative economy. Instead, its activities are carried out informally, shaped by historical tradition, dominated by the *grandes maisons* and by the manufacturing sector and artisanal workshops, but none of these provides support or an opportunity structure. There do not appear to be active links between the new independent initiatives and the bigger companies, other than that some of the new fashion microentrepreneurs might have spent time working for the well-known brands and subsequently been let go. We have had to look to regional studies and economic geography to find the perspectives needed to understand both the industry per se and the more widely scattered fashion start-ups and microenterprises.

The *milieu of labour*: Milan

Some of the thinking that informed the launch of the creative economy in the UK in 1997, when New Labour came to power, was informed by a set of Italian dialogues that had been carried out across the left–liberal spectrum of political and economic thinking from the mid-1980s onwards. In effect, 'designer culture' was imported from Italy to become an undergirding of the UK creative economy. These discussions took place in the UK in think-tanks like Demos and in academic circles involving sociologists and economists such as Stuart Hall, Martin Jacques and Robin Murray in the pages of various scholarly neo-Marxist journals.[7] In response to the long-drawn out crisis in the British economy from the mid-1970s, and especially the miners' strike of 1984, various left-wing authors turned to the Third Italy[8] and to the pioneering focus on small-scale fashion, textiles and clothing production units scattered across the originally artisanal workshops now connecting with each other on a regional basis in the form of 'districts' comprising 'not simply a local milieu, but a value chain and a wider institutional environment' (Dunford 2006: 36; see also Pollert 1988; Murray 1989b).

One such article, published in Hall and Jacques's edited *New Times* volume in 1989, was titled 'Benetton Britain', in which Murray (1989a) provides a detailed account of the innovative techniques used by the company based in the Treviso region of Northern Italy. This extensive system (led by companies like Benetton), which used emerging technologies to update older traditional processes for leather and silk, cotton and wool textiles, was seen as exemplifying the shift to a post-Fordist model of flexible production, one that fitted with the more differentiated consumer needs that, in turn, were being driven by the spectacular visibility of youth culture and the revolution in design and lifestyle (Murray 1989b). These tastes for distinctive and more highly styled products were regarded as offering a possible solution to the crisis of production in the advanced economies brought about by competition from both globalization and from the emerging economies operating with a low-cost labour market. Hence the look to Italy, which was seen to be leading the way by safeguarding its own core skills and expanding on this reputation through innovation, while also developing cost-cutting models in manufacture and production. The Third Italy came to inform and give shape to the UK's promotion of the creative industries by the late 1990s and early 2000s. The *New Times* volume, which reprinted articles from *Marxism Today* from the 1988–9 period, also included pieces by figures who went on, less than ten years later, to be leading lights in the Tony Blair-led government of 1997, and to become prominent champions of the new cultural economy.[9] The key feature of the Third Italy model that appealed to the New Labour government was the emphasis on energetic small-scale entrepreneurialism as well as on the use of new computerized technologies, such that the idea of 'innovation' took root. As Murray wrote in relation to Benetton, 'computers have been applied to design, cutting down the waste of materials and to stock control. Distribution has been revolutionised, as has the link between sales, production and innovation' (1989a: 57).

But how does this overlooked connection help us to understand the precarious situation of young designers in Italy, and in the Milan region in particular, today? It seems as if the 'miracle' of the Third Italy quite quickly faded; it was incapable of reproducing itself to bring on board a younger generation, while, conversely, what New Labour did with the heralding of the creative economy was to foreground young people. In Italy, an equivalent cohort of would-be creative professionals have had to come up with their own strategies to embark on a career in the creative field, without the support systems that have been put in place over two decades for their UK and German counterparts. This in turn raises the question of where we might locate that nexus of disciplinary/productive/capacity-generating activities operating in

a designated, if porous, environment, which we have designated the *milieu of labour*. If there is no single institutional
entity within which urban cultural policies are devised and
then implemented, arguably this gap is filled by the family
and a wide circle of friends, neighbours and the community,
and then by the wider cultural environment. This includes
the micro-activities of local, regional and national everyday
structures within which fashion and textile 'know-how'
exists as craft and tradition. It is also part of the heritage,
something that, if not passed on literally through families,
can be accessed in a community of expertise. This comprises,
for example, the local dressmaker, the leather workshop, the
boutique owner who designs and makes most of the items on
sale in her shop, or who agrees to take the selection of bags
created by the daughter of her neighbour. It also includes
dispersed figures such as the young woman, a fashion
graduate but currently unemployed, who makes wedding
dresses, or the young man trying his hand at tailoring or
the shirt-maker, and so on. 'The city itself is seen as part
of the cycle of production and as a resource constructed
by the accumulation of history, culture, tacit knowledge
and common channels of the peoples and institutions in the
territory' (Rullani 1997, quoted by Vanni 2016: 443).

This idea of fashion also functions as a kind of cultural
memory, resurrected with new life breathed into it by the
media campaign to promote 'Made in Italy'.[10] While there
are some attempts across the regions to develop a series of
job-creating urban arts and cultural policies, and in effect
to catch up with other countries in this regard, the slogan
fills the gap by making reference to the world-renowned
expertise in craft and fine goods including fashion and
textiles. Tradition and heritage are each invoked around the
signifier of Italianicity, and, with the ubiquity of the slogan,
there is the suggestion that the craft and artisanal workshops
are to be revived and brought back to life. This marks a
hoped-for turnaround and transition out of the now recognized limitations and failings of the Third Italy, as it faltered
under the pressure of globalization and the rise of financial
capitalism. We can trace just a thin line between this Made
in Italy initiative to remind the world about the high quality
and artisanship of Italian fashion, and the various attempts

by the young people we interviewed for this project to set themselves up in business in this overarching image of Italian high-quality production. Made in Italy occupies the same kind of polemical space more than twenty years later as the UK's 'talent-led economy' did from the late 1990s under the auspices of the New Labour government. It too marked a stage of capitalist development beyond post-Fordism. Since then, in both countries, and following on from the banking crisis of 2008, there has been a further ramping up of the neoliberalization of the economy through implementing harsh cuts to public spending. In Italy, there is a gradual recognition of the possible value of culture to the economy and, with this, a growth in new labour markets. But the dominant vocabulary is still governed by the importance of heritage. EU social projects foreground this emphasis on the built environment, ancient monuments, the museum sector and national galleries and their art work treasures. The dearth of policies for young people interested in fashion means that, from 2008 onwards, this generation is even more exposed to unemployment and to the precarity of casual jobs and unpaid internships. This lack of fashion policy infrastructure has arguably led to outcomes that also impinge on this current study (Belfiore 2004).

We might propose that the Third Italy actually sowed the seeds of what came to be the creative economy in the UK, and that, as the Third Italy in effect collapsed under the weight of rampant globalization and weak government, and as young people suffered under the impact of the 2008 financial crisis, those microenterprises that emerged in the Milan area bear witness to this double depletion of opportunities. Often, they have had to piggy-back on the outer edges of EU-funded social fund projects led by Brussels initiatives and overseen by multiple stakeholders, including university departments and local federations and trade associations as well as vocational education providers.[11] From under this weight, what appears is a scattered set of even smaller microenterprises than is seen in either of the other two cities in our study. What they share is an identity based on the artisanal tradition, Made in Italy. As noted above, the real irony here is that the figure of the 'fashion designer' as a person professionally skilled to create products not for luxury consumption, but for the new middle-class mass market (as exemplified in Benetton) was veritably imported from the Third Italy in the 1980s, and provided something of an inspiration among the progressive left in the UK from the mid-1980s on (and thus during the Thatcher years) for establishing a new post-Fordist consumer culture, and from here a pathway was created that led to the 'creative economy'.[12] Italy provided the original model for this whole edifice.[13] In what follows, we offer a brief overview of discussions among mostly economic geographers to assess our claim that the *milieu of labour* in Italy for the fashion sector comprises the idea of the family firm, enlarged to incorporate extended family, neighbourly contacts and the wider local community, which then finds expression in the Made in Italy slogan as a promotional device that also covers over the much thinner, indeed barely existing, policy infrastructure.

Benetton and beyond

At the heart of the Third Italy was the model forged by companies like Benetton, which grew out of a close-knit family of two brothers and a sister from a modest background in the Treviso region. This model, as it took on a more advanced character, combined various elements to create what appeared to be a distinctive and more modern post-Fordist mode of production. Eventually, the emphasis was on the idea of creating a popular global brand with a huge range of products available in a wide range of colours. (The word 'colour' was also a key part of the brand identity, as in the United Colours of Benetton.) To achieve this success, the company tapped into indigenous local craft and artisanal skills in small-scale, including homeworking, units, mostly for knitwear. At the same time, it used new computer-based technology especially developed to improve dyeing techniques. And then, with skilful advertising campaigns, the company invented a new young middle-class demographic that would buy into the mid-market brand on the basis of style and quality and a fast-changing range of products. This was achieved by linking a scattered set of production units dotted about the urban periphery with a core centre closer to the city (of Treviso) where dye technologies using advanced chemical processes allowed the company to introduce short runs and expand the wide colour palette of the knitwear and cotton collections. Post-Fordism worked at both sides of the production and consumption process, as customers saw the appeal of design and the rarity value of the short runs.[14] The company was able to cut costs by employing homeworkers (knitters and finishers and seamstresses) on a subcontractual basis. Benetton also plugged into the long-established Italian emphasis on regions for economic policymaking, which in turn was ramped up in the early 1980s in a series of deregulation moves by government that exempted small workshops and enterprises from stricter labour regulations and that awarded subsidies to small enterprises for taking on young people on a temporary basis.

In effect, this consolidated the importance of districts, and while fashion and clothing production has long been spread across the country (with different regions often specializing in different skills, such as leather in Tuscany or shirt-making in Naples), it was the northern Italy region that now moved more rapidly to a postindustrial economy. Benetton championed what was labelled the core and periphery model, with better-paid and more highly skilled workers, including designers and textile scientists, employed at the HQ, and with production carried out in small factories and on an artisanal basis. As mentioned above, Benetton placed great importance on the visual aspects of marketing and branding. Investments transformed the company into a global household name, while its franchise system of retail also cut employment costs. Most important was the emphasis on the 'designer' element. As Scott Lash and John Urry (1994) commented, post-Fordism saw an inversion of the old model of production such that the design studio became the centre of operations, with the small factory or homeworking unit receding into the background. 'Designer capitalism' was found in its most advanced forms in northern Italy, with design skills residing mostly in male hands and based more on an extension of artisanship and existing handed-down expertise than on a university training. Nor, at this stage, was the image of the haute couture designer so present; it was more like the designer as a highly skilled creative technologist. This new definition of the designer role, celebrated in the UK by the founder of the Habitat furniture stores Terence Conran, took a further turn in the UK fashion mass market with the opening of retail outlet NEXT in 1986, led by the designer entrepreneur George Davis (Nixon 1996). And from here, as discussed above, the new popular politics of consumer culture underpinned by this innovative model found itself being widely discussed and admired, if with some ambivalence, on the part of (among others) the progressive left, in particular the *Marxism Today* 'New Times' writers who were trying to counter the popularity of Thatcher's privatization policies by exploring the possibilities of a popular consumer culture that would reflect more diverse social identities.[15]

To understand better the interviews with our Italian respondents, the Italian context needs a little more clarification. Costis Hadjimichalis (2006), for instance, suggests that the 'new regionalism' that accompanied the rhetoric about the Third Italy was predicated on the short runs and constant turnover of new styles – i.e., flexible specialization (as described above with respect to Benetton) was overpromoted as a model of good practice. There were too many 'grandiose claims' made about new jobs, about the new artisanship and the potential for export and thus growth for the Italian economy. This overlooked the typically exploitative relations that underpinned the revival of the artisanal workshop, with women family members often working for free or for very little indeed, a point made forcefully by Andrew Ross (2004). These kinds of exploitative family relations were, claimed Hadjimichalis, buried under the idea of social capital that underpinned the networks of the district system. And enthusiasm for the Third Italy model (including on the part of the unions) drew attention away from the role of the informal economy. Instead, a lot of talk was about reviving the 'embedded tacit knowledge' of the artisan. This missed the point that, globally, the picture did not look very good for Italy, where labour costs were three times higher than elsewhere. It seems, then, that reawakening 'embedded tacit knowledge' only became possible some decades later, in an era of much lower incomes and during the precarious times that followed the financial crisis, when, as was the case for our contacts, working in a self-employment capacity as opposed to being unemployed made it easier for them to concentrate again on their craft and artisanal skills. Meanwhile, and in the context of globalization – especially for fashion – brand leaders and individual firms, for example Prada, were actually quite rapidly withdrawing from the famous districts, and finding various off-shore alternatives.

Made in Italy marks an attempt to reinvigorate the kinds of activities associated with the Third Italy, but in different and even more constrained economic circumstances. There is a paradox here because, despite the downturn in consumer spending from 2008 onwards, and the rise of fast fashion as strong competition to the Italian big brands alongside competition from other countries able to produce more goods more cheaply in many cheap labour countries, Italy still, as Ross (2004) points out, retains a leading position among the advanced economies for its fashion and textile manufacture and production. Thus, while the Third Italy lost its vanguard place, the global brands were able to remain at the forefront with their canny ability to produce cheaper diffusion lines, including tights and sunglasses.

The Third Italy collapsed quite quickly, in the space of six years from 1996 to 2002, with companies that had employed more than 6,000 workers just three or four years earlier having, following mergers and acquisitions, barely 400 employees on their books by the end of this period (Dunford 2006). By then, the fashion sector had almost fully succumbed to the dominant trends in political economy, from private equity buy-outs to the key roles played by finance capital and the futures market (Arvidsson and Malossi 2010). The neoliberal global economy pushed companies to look to Tunisia, Lithuania and Albania for cheaper factory production. It was only the final stages that were then assembled in microfactories in Tuscany, in particular in Prato, often employing Chinese sweated labour. Hadjimichalis (2006) punctures the rosy image of the Third Italy by making connections between past and present, reminding readers that moonlighting and informal labour had long been a characteristic of local district-based production. The informal economy had also been able to sweep up and conceal higher rates of especially male unemployment than had been associated with the Third Italy, as the bigger companies began to look abroad for cheaper labour at every stage of the production process. 'The supposed unbroken tradition of making things by hand in artisanal workshops from the Renaissance until today does not make sense when the value of the products produced in Italy is only 15–45%' (Ross 2004: 210). Not only did this district-led system meet its virtual demise as a result of competition from abroad, but so also did local high-skilled labour begin to dry up as young people left the small towns and villages in search of a future in what they perceived as the more glamourous areas of the fashion industry, such as fashion communications, marketing, photography and PR. From this perspective, the image of the Third Italy that inspired the UK creative economy was wildly optimistic.

Michael Dunford confirms this shift, making the case that indeed, for the Italian textiles and clothing industry, what counts now is the increasingly decentralized firm pushing ahead on the basis of delocalization and outsourcing. The district model became outmoded by the end of the twentieth century, such that making sense of Italian fashion requires a focus on the financial power of the global brands. Instead of districts, Dunford cites the idea of a wider 'magic circle' of companies, with Milan at its centre and increasingly inhabited by many young professionals: designers, showroom managers, retailers and boutique owners, agents, photographers, social media workers, fashion writers, stylists, make-up artists, graphic designers, etc., all scattered across the city and into its outskirts. This comes about in conjunction with the virtual collapse of textile production and the attendant loss of jobs. There is then a shift away from the very small workshops and units of production spread across the periphery, to arrangements where specialism still exists in name (leather in Tuscany, silk in Como, wool in Treviso, etc.), but the main elements of the manufacturing and production work are carried out abroad, leaving significant numbers of young people in the city and its surrounding small towns hoping for an exciting job in the fashion world of Milan, but without the existence of a government-led creativity *dispositif* and hence without the policy infrastructure that might formalize or regularize the proliferation of informal economic activities. These are mostly graduates living a hand-to-mouth existence and reliant on unpaid internships and temporary employment in the hope of gaining a foothold in big fashion companies like Prada or Gucci or Jil Sander, etc.

Female-led artisanship: Milanese small-scale fashion production

> I wanted to become a fashion designer since I was seven ... I wanted to go to a fine art high school and that caused a small tragedy in my family! After school, I enrolled in the Marangoni Institute to study fashion design. I liked it but what I could never understand was why we were encouraged to design clothes that were impossible to wear. At one point I went into a crisis, as I really felt different from what they seemed to expect me to be ... I was not interested in all the glamorous world of impossible clothes, I was inspired by the more artisanal side of fashion, the very 'making' side of it. (Interview with Camilla Vinciguerra, BeConvertible, July 2014)

> 'Made in Italy' is a guarantee of good fabrics, accurate tailoring and personal delivery through boutiques and specialised shops. (Mora 2006: 349)

There has been an upsurge in academic interest in cultural labour and new research since the 2010s that in Italy has led to a creative economy agenda.[16] Mostly this comes from economic and cultural geographers but also, more widely, from sociologists and a small number of fashion theorists most of whom we have already referred to – e.g., Laura Bovone, Carolina Bandinelli, Emanuela Mora, Marianna D'Ovidio, Marc Pradel, Adam Arvidsson, Enrico Bertacchini, Paola Borrione, Paolo Volonte, Francesco Capone and Luciana Lazaretti among others (see also Mole 2010; Montalto 2010). These theorists anticipate an expansion in this field of activity and provide a series of templates for future work. There is a double ambition, both to legitimize creative industry studies and to urge professionals in policymaking and urban planning to follow suit. The words 'urban creative economy' have the ability to give a title and a shape to more scattered or 'disorganized' activities and thus enable a process of institutional consolidation to begin in the universities and, more widely, beyond. After all, there are many professionals in the field who move constantly between three sites: universities, town halls and the media. The investigation by D'Ovidio and Pradel of the Isola della Moda project is particularly useful because of its focus on the fashion activities that came into being around the initiatives that began in 2004–5 (D'Ovidio and Pradel 2013; Raunig 2013).

The Isola della Moda was an example of autonomous and 'bottom-up' organization on the part of young fashion professionals who were experiencing hardship and high levels of unemployment and who were also excluded from the nepotistic recruitment of the dominant fashion houses in Milan. Over a short time, a small group of alternative fashion designers developed a system for mentoring, for offering production support, and the opportunity to sell designer items from the shop they opened up in the Isola neighbourhood (formerly an industrial but now out-of-use space just five kilometres from the city centre). D'Ovidio and Pradel (2013) point out that the fashion designers had little real contact, or any way of engaging, with the 'dense networks' of the powerful fashion companies that nevertheless made Milan 'one of the world capitals of fashion'. The fashion houses were seen as impenetrable, with their 'locked networks'. The exclusive stance of the Camera Nazionale della Moda (National Chamber of Italian Fashion) meant that, in reality, the big brands were not tuned into innovation and creativity, 'fashion did not appear to be an asset for the city as a whole' (Arvidsson et al. 2011). The Isola della Moda therefore offered an experimental space to counter the exclusive and closed-door image of the fashion houses, generating enthusiasm as well as laying the groundwork for a critical practice that emphasized environmental values of sustainability as the defining features of the alternative model of fashion production. The work entailed a 'rediscovery of the traditional elaboration methods ... for a different point of view for fashion ... from the circuit of large firms' (quoted by D'Ovidio and Pradel 2013). But without support from the local municipality, participants found themselves reliant on family support not just for bed and board, but also for much more, including childcare.

They relied on 'family solidarity', 'the typical Italian inter-generational support'. This dependency factor confirms the lack of proactive cultural policies directed at the creative cohort in the city and more widely in Italy. This account by D'Ovidio and Pradel corresponds almost exactly with the key themes in the interviews carried out for our CREATe project.

We observed a feminist-inspired revival of the artisan tradition, despite the obstacles, and in conditions of hardship that make their outcomes, pathways and survival uncertain.[17] London, by contrast, was looked to as a beacon of opportunity. As one young designer put it: 'The dream would be Brick Lane.' What we see in the interviews below are young people reworking small-scale craft enterprises by taking things into their own hands. Instead of the old male-dominated artisanal workshops, they now operate in brightly lit and tastefully decorated fashion studios. With the support of family or spouses, these workers suggest 'gendered social innovation' (Lindberg et al. 2015). The skill set is upgraded to match the art school training and the higher levels of education of these young designers. As the comment from Camilla Vinciguerra, quoted at the top of this section, shows, the family of this young woman had higher expectations for her than a career in fashion. Artisanship seemed like a step down. However, her perseverance paid off. Her studio, which originally belonged to her mother, was transformed into a stylish space.

As our field notes show: 'Camilla is dressed casually, with high waist black trousers and a yellow vest. Her long hair tied in a soft tress. When I arrived there, I was immediately offered fresh water, berries and a cigarette. When I complimented her nice atelier, she told me: "I do it to express myself" as if to justify herself, or at least to clarify an important point.' After graduating, Camilla had jobs with well-known companies in Milan and found that her interest was drawn to tailoring and, alongside this, to manufacturing. Her second job was with a company making bags – 'and with this I got to know about leather'. At a later stage, she realized that she could possibly start designing and making bags herself. She went to a leather fair in Bologna, bought some pieces and got in contact with someone she knew who had a leather workshop. She made a few samples and immediately sold them to friends. At this stage she impressed her mother with this new activity. Her mother offered studio space and went on to help her in the business with administrative support. Friends and extended family provided further support, including help with accountancy and with promotional videos. To begin with, they did this for free, but later she was able to pay for this help to grow the business.

Camilla also enjoyed talking about her range of bags and how they filled a vacuum in the market for travel. She had developed a technique that meant her range could be customized and thus marketed as unique at the point of sale. The ideal consumer, as stated in our interview, was a young business woman: 'BeConvertible (my label) is thought to meet the needs of strong women, with versatile needs, a dynamic life, they are bags you can fit a notebook in, they're like a briefcase for women.'

Camilla expressed a preference for e-commerce and for developing sales across the world. She saw the limitations in selling in shops in Italy because they were too driven by the big brand names in a way she found 'snobbish'. She also had a strong awareness of those aspects of the fashion industry that she did not want her own collection of bags to be associated with, such as fast fashion and the unrealistic avant-garde of high-end fashion. Most important from our perspective is that, not only had Camilla brought in her mother, but also her sister, who designed and made shoes. These women were taking up the reins left behind by the older generation of men in the artisanal workshop.

> For us is a family philosophy, my sister produces shoes, and follows the same values, she makes a long-lasting product! Fashion mirrors the times, and now you cannot think of a consumer culture as it was in the eighties. I think things are changing, I feel part of a bigger movement of like-minded independent fashion designers. (Interview, November 2014)

Our next interview also concerns a woman entrepreneur who launched her own fashion company in 2012/13. Denise Bonapace had previously worked as a designer for two major companies and was also teaching part time at the Politecnico.

Two years ago I decided to set up my own business. To do things differently. With a very small initial investment. Now we are three: me, a girl who does communication, and a guy who manages the contact with the sellers. At the moment I have managed to be sustainable, but I have not made any profit. In the next years I hope this may become my main job. I do not want to be rich, just to turn it into my job. My main job. Of course for living now I still do consultancies, and I teach as well. (Interview, July 2014)

Denise shared with Camilla a similar critique of the fashion industry: the shops only wanted big brands and the big brands were dominated by the seasonal calendar and a throwaway ethos. Being independent brought the freedom to invent new ways for doing fashion: 'I do not follow the trends, I do not use the fashionable colours, I am not driven by marketing research but by creativity, ideas and exploration'. She continued at length, explaining how she worked:

The problem of fashion nowadays, of both luxury brands and fast fashion, is that designers are commanded by marketing. Research is driven by the marketing department, not by the designers. The marketing department does research on what products sell the most and then designers are presented with a number of items they have to produce ... In fast fashion companies the situation is even worse. Designers working for ZARA are required to constantly design thousands of clothes. It is a mass scale production of conformist products. There's no room for creativity and research.

Denise is part of a new, more feminist-aware generation as she talks about the straitjacket of the mainstream fashion industry:

Now at the Politecnico we are doing a project on old people's bodies ... that does not mean only designing dresses for old people, but also getting inspired by different needs and shapes, different bodies. Thinking of how an old person moves, I can find a way to do a better sleeve, a more comfortable one ... The body of the elderly is the extreme antithesis of the fashion body, that is why it is so tremendously interesting.

This radical spirit has also led to ideas about setting up a more cooperative model for people who share similar ideas.

I am thinking of setting up a consortium of like-minded independent fashion designers, who have the same ideas and values ... of making a sustainable and democratic fashion that escapes the diktat of marketing. I believe in the power of making a difference, even with small things, or starting with small things.

Denise encompasses two of our designated 'ideal type' factors for Italy: she takes part in some of the radical alternative projects and, at the same time, she uses the label of being an independent female designer committed to sustainability to carve out a space for herself, which is at variance with the big business models that dominate the Milan scene.

Of course, then the problem is that if you produce unique pieces, high quality, and do everything in Italy, as I do, the costs are high, and the shops take a big slice too, so in the end a knitwear of mine can cost 400 euros, which is a foolish price ... But there's no way out of this ... I have discussed it with many colleagues and at the moment I cannot see a way to change it ...

All the big brands, they put the label 'Made in Italy', but they produce abroad. The law allows it; basically it is enough if you do the sampling here, relying on high-quality manufacturing, especially in Tuscany, and then you outsource the production, and then you sew the label here and that's it: it's 'Made in Italy'.

Similar themes appeared in our interview with Ela Siromacenco (Elochka.com). Originally from Romania, she had a story like Camilla's – she had to battle with her parents to be allowed to study fashion, since they regarded it as a low-skill and too traditional sector for an ambitious young woman, so instead she studied marketing to PhD level and then returned to her ideas about setting up with her own designs. She started selling them on etsy.com in 2012. 'I remember my parents were always telling me: You don't have to sew! You have to study!'

Ela was very open about the bad state of the labour market in Milan for graduates like herself:

In early 2012, I got my PhD and started to look for a job. That was terrible! It was just impossible! There were just no jobs out there for me ... In the vast majority of cases I didn't even get a reply ... I felt really depressed, and useless. I did not know what to do really ... I actually applied even for quite bad jobs, like call centres and stuff, this is to say I was not choosy at all, and I have a PhD! I mean ... I was quite qualified ... but no way. (Interview, July 2014)

Ela made a few dresses that sold on Etsy, and she then started to study fashion more seriously with online courses:

Then I decided to seriously invest in this project, and bought my first industrial sewing machine. I designed my first small collection, mainly '50s-style dresses. I like the style of the '50s, and also I realized there could have been a market for them. It is a niche market of course, but it is niche markets that work well.

And so here I am! And next season I will present my first full collection, inspired by Naples. I work a lot ... I work all the time. I do everything by myself ... that cannot be sustainable for a long time ... I hope to be soon able to hire someone to help me!

I don't have any contact with the so-called Milan fashion scene. I guess I am a free-rider, something of an outsider. I just design and sew in my room, and then I sell the dresses all over the world exploiting the opportunities offered by the internet. This is it. I have not grown up here, I have not gone to the hype schools like IED, Politecnico or Marangoni. Therefore, I really don't know everyone, I am not involved in any kind of network. I just do things by myself, and this is it.

So these are niche small-scale activities, with each woman pursuing a determined pathway and managing to draw on the image of Italy and Milan as globally renowned fashion centres and to create their own Made in Italy identity, which means drawing attention to the distinctive high-quality features of their work.

Ela continued to describe how her business model worked in practice

In 2013, to set up my enterprise I invested 5000 euros, in 2014 my turnover was 17,000 euros ... I am investing every-thing so actually I have not made any profit yet. I have paid myself a salary of 500 euros per month, and have spent a lot of money, you have to consider that the costs I have for the enterprise and ... for my life, actually the two are one ... my life is not separated from my work.

If it wasn't for the opportunities offered by e-commerce I wouldn't have been able to set up a business ... Had I had to open a shop, pay the rent, invest in advertising, it would have been just impossible. Also, if I had to sell my stuff to other shops, instead of having my own, it would have still been very hard because I would have had to sell my creations at a much higher price ... and for a new brand it is hard to sell expensive things and to immediately compete with big players.

She carried on to explain her own marketing strategy: 'The benefit of selling online is that you can reach a super-wide audience ... I do mostly dresses, and wedding dresses, and the fact that somewhere in the world is always summer is a very important advantage for me! When in Italy nobody gets married, in Australia everyone does!'

A similar pathway was seen for the business couple, under the label of Matthan Gori, who specialized in haute couture items, especially wedding dresses. Matthan came from Istanbul and moved to Milan to the Politecnico, with fashion being more acceptable to his parents than acting, which was his original idea.

I studied fashion at the Politecnico, and before finishing I did an internship in a fashion firm. I was shocked, because it was a period of crisis, there were many layoffs, and I used to see employees just praying that they would not lose their job ... Then I thought, if I need to pray, then I want to pray for my job! Not for someone else's!

He continued:

But how can one get into the fashion world? Either you do showroom or on consignment, but it doesn't work unless you're a friend of Donatella Versace. Fashion shops just don't create space for young stylists ...

What I like about my job is the relationship with the clients ... And because we make the dress you wear on the most important day of your life. Well you know ... we play a very important role! Wedding dress are exclusive ... There are still brides who call us, who invite us for dinners ... My pictures are in many family photo albums!

> I have to say I felt more of an entrepreneur than a designer ... I prefer much more the entrepreneurial aspects ... Taking decisions for the brand, you know, I decide everything for Matthan Gori. I like to think about the future of the brand, how to hit new markets, how to design a second line ... This is creative, to create something out of nothing is creative. My creation is Matthan Gori, not the single dresses.

The two young women who started Flatwig did so on an even slimmer basis than our other respondents. They are graduates in architecture and were jobless when they began to make a few pieces of minimalist jewellery that were quickly snapped up by friends, with requests for more pieces. As Erica Agogiati, co-founder of Flatwig, said:

> Then we started thinking of a brand. We are aware that branding is very important nowadays, so we thought about the brand and the products at the very same time. We got inspiration from various sources, mainly the Pink Floyd, Formafantasma [a creative design studio based in Amsterdam and led by an Italian duo] and to start Flatwig we invested something like 500 euros ... very low budget! Our products are low cost, consider that a ring costs 5–6 euro, and we sell it at 7,90.
>
> So we need to sell a lot ... we want to go to designer markets ... the dream would be Brick Lane! And to sell online. Next thing, we will open a shop on Etsy, it costs 20 cents for each product you upload, for four months, plus the 3.5% on the sales ... So it is very doable. We are learning how to be entrepreneurs ... We don't know how it'll go ... But the point is now we're happy! ... We feel like working but we don't feel the burden ... if we won't go on holiday, who cares! And at parties we can say truthfully that we are designers.

The Flatwig young women most clearly expressed their relief about being busy and having found something meaningful to do. Their comments more substantially reflect the emphasis by writers like Franco Berardi (2009) on how the impact of the financial crisis and exponentially high unemployment amongst graduates creates an epidemic of depression and mental health crises. This kind of activity and the plans they see emerging from a very basic model of entrepreneurship widen their horizons, and they can see a better future appear. The more emotive tone that runs through these comments shows the toll of being either unemployed or on the edges of employment.

Another female duo, Antonella Bellina and Elisa Fregna (DueDiLatte), developed an equally distinctive product and identity, again from a small starting point. They had been employed in a design company in Milan, but were frustrated at the slow pace and lack of innovation. They felt stifled and that their ideas were not being taken on board:

> *Antonella*: I had worked with milk fibre for other brands, but besides this I had done a lot of research by myself and found out the potential of the milk fibre. I had had this idea for a while but I knew I couldn't develop it on my own, also because I don't have all the skills you need to run a company. Therefore I asked Elisa, who is good at marketing, and I thought our skills could be complementary.
>
> *Elisa*: Yes. One morning, during a lunch break, we were complaining about the job, about how the company was dealing with things ... we were saying that their approach needed to be changed but that nobody would have ever done it. What we didn't like about the company we were working for is that they would never risk, never innovate, they were bound by an old way of doing things. In particular, they would try to save money by outsourcing the production to find a cheap labour force, therefore the result was that the products were not really high quality ... and also they did not invest in online marketing at all ... this is ridiculous! Times have changed and the old class of entrepreneurs simply don't realize it!
>
> *Antonella*: Moreover, really, this thing of saving on the labour force brings low quality, you have t-shirts that, once washed, are useless! Everybody wants to spend less and less but then you have just crap products. You have shoes whose soles just burn your feet if you walk for more than an hour!

This business model developed by the two young women drew on various criticisms they had of the mainstream fashion industry. As Elisa said: 'We do things differently, we want to make a quality product. But then of course our prices are higher, one of our t-shirts may be sold for 75 euros, we're talking boutiques in which the other t-shirts may cost even 230, so we're still the basic line!'

Elisa also had a realistic vision of what was involved in setting up as an independent label:

> If you want to do this career, then you have to face many diffi-culties, it's a very precarious situation ... the entrepreneurial aspect is crucial. We were used to work the long hours ... and we have grown up in a job market that requires flexibility, so in a sense we were prepared, but still ... When you are an entrepreneur you have all the responsibility, you pay for all your mistakes ... you have to deal with many different aspects ... with the finance, funding. You have to try to be long-sighted ...
>
> We are trying to do things ethically, and to produce a good product, high quality. Our innovation is the milk fibre. Besides this, we are developing our brand identity. In the future we would like to have our own e-commerce. As for now, we are focusing more on our offline network, we are trying to create good relationships with produces and retailers in the territory.

There is, throughout these interviews (all conducted in July 2014) an informal and experimental 'try it out' ethos based on some 'feel' for small-scale entrepreneurship. Not all the respondents talked about artisanship, but the idea of being able to acquire the right kind of skills to participate meaningfully in fashion suggested a familiarity with the values of high-quality craftsmanship as something that could be literally seen around them in the towns, cities and villages across the country. The culture of fashion, then, in Italy is ordinary, a feature of everyday life, rather than something exceptional. For this young generation, setting up with an independent label stemmed from a perceived and typically experienced dissatisfaction with the state of the fashion industry in Italy and also their desire to find a more authentic way of working, one that somehow reflected their own value systems and beliefs. Still, these biographical narratives also reveal how hard it is to keep going when the de facto *milieu of labour* is the institutional nexus of the immediate and extended family and the local community.

Conclusion

The young women (and two men) whom we interviewed are different from the designers we spoke to in London and Berlin. They are not prize-winners and they have not developed a big name for themselves in the city. The system in Italy does not work in a way that would easily allow young unknowns to emerge into the spotlight. This would only be possible for someone who came from an already established wealthy fashion family.[18] In their search for new talent, the fashion houses look instead to prize-winners from the UK, where the groundwork has already been laid by the London fashion colleges and the magazines and press, as well as by social media promoting these new names.[19] This explains how, despite being in the same city, a large chasm separates the mainstream industry from these young fashion designers working on a much smaller, almost DIY scale. Given this seemingly unpropitious situation, what gives these young people a sense of purpose is that they are somehow part of Italy's world-renowned fashion industry. They can tap into this history. More concretely, they can take into their own hands a rich history of production and artisanship. They can access reliable sources of fabrics, often at cost price, and they can find out about the equipment they need by plugging into local networks. They can combine the old with the new, gaining access to customers through online platforms, and it is this dimension that makes their entrepreneurial activity most distinctive. They have merged a craft ethos with the artisanship and the know-how prised out of male hands and now implanted into these more feminized atelier spaces. We could describe this informal scene as one dominated by young women, mostly graduates, coming forward and creating jobs for themselves in a wider environment where, despite this being a fashion city in a country where the fashion and textiles industries have for decades been leading sectors and major contributors to GDP, there has been an absence of proactive policies (for example, aiming at getting more women into work) coming from either regional or national governments. And this is also a context that has been male-dominated from top to bottom, so the gender reversal that is happening is suggestive of a force for change and the emphasis by young women on their urgent need for economic independence through the unleashing of their wage-earning capacity, even if in adverse economic circumstances.

The big brands appear to be aloof and untouched by social issues and by ongoing political debate about high unemployment rates among young people. They did not seem to grant the independent fashion microentrepreneurs in Italy the kind of significance that their London counterparts have been given (on the basis of the reputation of both CSM and LCF). Nor do they seem tuned into any benefits that might be accrued from their developing more socially inclusive perspectives. Not only did the young DIY designers have to define their own pathways, but, especially for young women, they had to counter the lingering image of sewing or 'dressmaking' as traditional, low-status fields belonging to the female homeworking or outsourcing tradition. This is a feminist issue. The family business ethos (the *milieu of labour*) has allowed young women to emerge with their own independent labels, yet this reflects and confirms their dependency on the family, or on a husband or partner and his or her extended family, to provide various forms of support to get the microenterprise off the ground. Whether it is childcare or rent-free home space to work in and live in, this is a double-edged form of support and one that may not be available to those from low-income backgrounds, and especially for those unable to remain in the family home. We end this chapter reflecting on a *milieu of labour* that is informal and based on local knowledge. The middle-class family rather than the social institutions hold this together. Gradually, and perhaps more noticeably during and after the pandemic, the various well-funded Fondazione (often serving as the charitable wing of family-owned companies) have developed initiatives to support artists, designers and other cultural producers. There have been calls for competitive bids.[20] The strongest non-family agencies are, however, the universities and art schools, perhaps also social science departments, where a new feminist sociology of fashion might lead to a wider public debate about how to marry a strong feminist ethos for female employment and good jobs for women with the ambition to reform and indeed transform the fashion sector.

5

Click and Collect: Fashion's New Political Economy

Introduction: The new political economy

This chapter asks the following questions: how does the rapid growth of fashion-tech and e-commerce alter the landscape of fashion culture today? Do these phenomena necessitate adjustment to the main concept introduced so far in this book, notably the *milieu of labour*? Why, when our focus has been on fashion microenterprises, is it important to reflect on the digital pathways of both the luxury brands and the fast fashion companies? And what impact do these changes have on the independent sectors of activity in London, Berlin and Milan? In this chapter, we look at how these changes across the whole sector reflect on the designers we interviewed for this study, and we conclude with three fashion-tech case studies. One involves interviews with employees of an Italian fast fashion company based in Milan, and the other two concern a feminist ethical not-for-profit label Birdsong and, in contrast, a more commercial, venture capital funded platform, Not Just A Label (NJAL). The case study from the larger fast fashion company provides an insight into future investigations of the new landscape of fashion labour processes. So far, labour theorists have studied working life and conditions at mega-companies like Amazon, but not as yet the fashion workforces for companies like Zalando or

ASOS. The methodologies used for this chapter extend those developed for the previous chapters, with some amendments. We asked the independent designers in the three cities for updates as they made more and more use of e-commerce, exacerbated by the global pandemic of 2020–22. The young people in Milan who had found work at a leading online fashion company (to which we are giving the name Ajax) provided us with detailed accounts of their working schedules by Zoom interview in late 2019, and we had already, earlier on in the research, met with and followed closely the activities of Birdsong, which is London-based, and also of Not Just A Label, which, in the course of our research, moved its location to Los Angeles as London rents for premises became unaffordable. The timespan for the research presented here is from 2015 to 2021 and the investigations overall are more hybrid, experimental and hence tentative than in the previous chapters.

Across the spectrum of fashion-tech operations, there is a constant round of buy-outs, mergers and changes in ownership. Underpinning the various acquisitions is the financial model of venture capital. No sooner is one deal announced than another take-over and merger of the same bunch of companies follows, so that it becomes difficult to track and pin down what is actually going on (which of course may be part of the mystifying logic of finance capital). Amazon is the major force of e-commerce in the West, but it has struggled to function as a fashion e-retailer, even though, as John Fernie and David Grant (2019) describe, it bought the exceptionally successful US shoe retailer Zappos.com in 2008 on the basis of its annual turnover of $1.1 billion. Zalando in Berlin was, for a period of time, Germany's top earning company, and its history is relevant to our study in that it developed strategies for e-commerce in relatively standard and male-oriented goods such as shoes and t-shirts.[1] It then extended into women's wear, mostly cheap fast fashion. Another German company, Mytheresa, this time a high fashion business, and based in Munich, came into being at the very start of the fashion-tech era, and was taken over in 2014 by the US luxury retail store Neiman Marcus, which also owned Bergdorf Goodman. Following the bankruptcy of Neiman Marcus, Mytheresa was lifted out of the bankrupt estate with loans and then, under the new ownership of MYT Netherlands, it was valued at $2.2 billion on the New York Stock Exchange (NYSE) in January 2021. Farfetch, one of the leading companies in fashion-tech, was launched in 2008 by Portuguese entrepreneur José Neves. A decade later it was valued on the NYSE at $5.8 billion, but then lost its high value through one acquisition (Off White) that failed to take off, but offset that with a buy-out of the upscale boutique Browns of London, so that by 2021 the company was employing 5,400 people with offices in Portugal, Chile, Italy and Brazil, as well as London. Neves reported a pre-tax loss of $3.35 billion for 2020, but expressed his hopes for a profit in 2021, following $1.1 billion further investment from Alibaba in China and Richemont in Switzerland (Moules 2021). The company is one of the UK's most valuable internet businesses, whose IPO was recently quoted at more than £5 billion.

The scale of the restructures and the movement of CEOs as reported on a daily basis by online journals such as www.businessoffashion.com (BoF) indicates the speculative character of fashion-tech as a futures market. Money amounting to billions of dollars, euros and pounds moves around the whole sector on a daily basis. New ventures are announced, to be quietly shut down only months later.[2] Amid this fashion-tech scramble, the UK occupies an important position. This is the case from both high-end and mainstream to fast fashion. The luxury designer site Net-a-Porter (with its later offshoots The Outnet, Mr Porter and then a glossy magazine *Porter*) was the fashion-tech leader, set up and overseen by the fashion entrepreneur Natalie Massenet, who was able to expand the company by attracting large sums of venture capital. This was the key platform for selling upmarket designer collections, and the expensive customer service online extended to tasteful packaging and special delivery by small customized black vans bearing the discrete and elegant Net-a-Porter logo.[3] The company has never made a profit (attributed to the need for investment in new tech and social media) and eventually Massenet was pushed out after the company was taken over in 2015 by the Italian fashion online company YOOX. YOOX Net-a-Porter has never been a household name, but it was able to raise 550 million euros to spend on technology, warehouses and delivery systems, as well as opening up a central London office at White City. Massenet moved to Net-a-Porter's key rival in the luxury fashion market, Farfetch. In the luxury field of vintage e-commerce, the French company Vestiaire Collective has also joined this elite circle. Its owners were able to raise $200 million of capital on selling just 5 per cent of the company to Kering. The overall value is now set at more than $1 billion, listing 140,000 new (vintage) items per week (Peter 2021).[4] MatchesFashion, another high-end fashion company, was sold in September 2017 for £1 billion to a private equity firm called Apax Partners. Both YOOX Net-a-Porter and MatchesFashion run their own logistics units, and have their own warehouses, while, by contrast, Farfetch makes its money by taking a 25 or 30 per cent commission on the sales it generates on its site.[5]

ASOS has become the largest online fast fashion and beauty retailer in the UK. By 2017, it was offering 85,000 different products and 4,000 styles each week to 12.4 million consumers. In 2021, it bought out the bankrupted Topshop, transferring all its sales to online only. The gamble of having no stores has paid off, especially during the pandemic. In July 2021, Gap announced the closure of all its stores in the UK. ASOS has made great efforts to improve its reputation for good practice in manufacture and production, in terms of both its workforce and its environmental obligations. Most recently, this entails creating a boost to UK employment, promising 2,000 new jobs with a planned opening of a giant £90 million warehouse in Staffordshire, having seen profits of £142 million following a surge of online sales due to Covid.[6] Fast fashion generally used to mean companies like Zara, which had mastered a range of techniques such as immediate feedback from shop-floor staff on customer trends and preferences, a sophisticated just-in-time system, a huge team of 700 in-house designers and with all production carried out in neighbouring regions, including ten logistics centres (which eventually accounted for such success that their owner for a short while was named as the richest person in the world). However, the notion of 'fast' has now shifted to delivery times rather than the speed at which new catwalk-copied styles can appear on the store rails. Already by 2017, fast fashion companies that were store-based were beginning to see their profits drop and their shares lose value, and meanwhile Zalando was offering free delivery and returns policies that allowed customers to send back their goods weeks after receiving them. By 2021, NEXT vans had words on their sides promising customers that they could 'order at midnight' and have their goods 'delivered by midday'. This then becomes a matter of delivery systems and what that requires of the workforce. Fashion-tech has become a major part of the gig economy, comprising zero hours contracts, low wages and poor working conditions. In this respect, it is playing a leading role in the degradation of labour.

The biggest and most powerful companies are, however, struggling to maintain the kind of profits required by their shareholders, and even when this is translated into notional values on futures markets, there are still signs that the high fashion or luxury sector could crumble. Famous fashion brands such as Armani and Gucci, and the kinds of labels that pride themselves on their Bond Street and Mayfair addresses in London, are struggling to find ways to duplicate the attentive luxury treatment given to wealthy customers, since it is this that enhances the value of the items on sale. Without this, they are at risk of losing their lustre. This loss is accompanied by further social media disruptors, most markedly the shift away from hard copy magazines and newspapers to the range of internet websites, including Instagram. No longer are the established fashion journalists the gatekeepers of luxury value, pointing their upmarket readers to the relevant boutiques. Now, old and new generations of consumers alike look to the bloggers and influencers whose ideas are less tied to luxury shopping areas. This is the context in which the big companies are forced to develop strategies to maintain control, in particular recruiting chief digital officers from companies such as Apple and Google.

The major labels are challenged by the need to maintain dominance and visibility in this social media space; meanwhile, there is also the risk of losing some of their wealthy consumers. This can be rationalized in conventional terms as the need to keep up with youth culture, the need to become more diverse and to gain new kinds of presence, but in the process there is a sense that the consumer demographic that could be relied on is slipping out of the grasp of fashion houses such as Prada, Gucci, Dolce e Gabbana, Armani, etc. The entire ecology of the fashion media has changed, and the *grandes maisons* are having to throw money in many directions to keep abreast. (In particular, they are using consultants to advise on race and ethnicity and on how to reach the TikTok generation.) New technologies have transformed the way in which fashion carries out its business. Instagram has pushed the industry to present a friendlier, less aloof and hierarchical face. The Instagram founder commented that the app 'shifts fashion from being this very detached, glossy magazine experience, it becomes more lived in … I think it connects to what people actually experience day-to-day, which is not the runway show. It's just life and life elevated.' And according to Eva Chen, head of fashion at Instagram, 'authenticity wins' (Armstrong 2016). What we can see then is that fashion-tech forces the up-market fashion scene to relinquish many of the exclusive cultural values that have shaped its institutions and its everyday life as a global business. E-commerce has also done away with the idea of retail as a personal service once the buying experience becomes a more privatized at-home activity, followed up with the delivery of a dress that may or may not become a 'return'. As we shall see in the next section, all of this has consequences for employment. The social setting for consumption and the leisure experience of a day out shopping are largely replaced by online communities, by the sociality of receiving personal emails and friendly recommendations. This all takes place in a context where financial capital swoops in and decides which of the various fashion-tech gadgets or apps might have lasting value on a scale that would bring windfalls and rewards to owners and shareholders. The fact that second-hand or vintage sites have recently attracted such vast sums from companies such as Etsy, which bought Depop for $1.62 billion in June 2021, suggests that the Silicon Valley ethos based on analytics and algorithms has quite profoundly landed on this sector. The new political economy is volatile and capricious. It can take huge risks with investment and see losses mount up, while also pursuing the demographic that promises the greatest rewards. Facing the challenges posed by the widespread critiques of the sector by young climate activists, the big companies for the first time in recent history feel themselves to be embattled and forced to review their operations at every level. And yet what is noticeably missing is the idea of supporting young independent designers in more significant ways, such as the provision of space, more widely available systems of mentorship or guidance, and support for managing e-commerce transactions. This reflects the absence of an influential fashion policymaking forum. The big companies are let off the hook in this respect, and independent designers are left to develop their own individual pathways through the digital landscape, with all that this entails.

The new world of 'listing labour'

The rise of e-commerce in fashion (as in other sectors) means geographical displacement and reconfiguration of the workforce. This too has consequences for the small independent fashion labels. In the big department stores, in concession areas and in other exclusive outlets (traditionally female) staff are losing their jobs at every level. Expertise on the part of buying teams is lost.[7] The shift to online fashion also sees a seismic increase in transportation and delivery, as well as in warehouse work and packaging. This is generally low-paid and relatively low-skill work, contributing overall to what we have called the 'degradation of labour'. Since this is both a recent and an unfolding phenomenon, sociological research on these topics remains sketchy. Economic geographers Fernie and Grant (2019) provide a useful overview of logistical fashion with reference to two major players, luxury brands and fast fashion, introducing key technical terms such as 'supply chain management', 'omnichannel retail' (i.e., buying from the various devices), 'third party logistics' (i.e., outsourced product delivery systems), 'pure players' (no stores at all), 'warehouse management systems' and 'online fulfilment centres' or 'dark stores'. And Ned Rossiter provides an account of the disciplining and down-skilling of the workforce.

> Within the space of warehouses and transport industries, the movement of workers is increasingly regulated by global

positioning system (GPS) vehicle tracking, radio-frequency identification tags that profile workers within database time and voice-directed order picking technologies ... The automated coordination and control of workers results in higher levels of productivity accompanied by increased demands and pressures upon the labouring body. Such technologies of governance correspond with the rise of what I would term 'informatized sovereignty', which takes on particular hues in logistical techniques associated with transportation industries. Code is King. (2014: 68)

Both of these accounts correspond with everyday observations about delivery systems, from the fleets of DPD and Hermes vans that appear round every corner in cities across the world, to the dominance of delivery systems by DHL at all times of day and night, to the various other forms of 'click and collect' that have been in place for several years. There are now many collect stations, from corner shops, to newsagents, to department stores like Karstadt in Berlin which, counterintuitively, allows its own customers to collect their Amazon parcels on the top floor alongside customer services and the restaurant. Collect stations like Doddle first appeared at busy train stations and then spread to high streets. Customers pay a small charge for the service per item or a monthly fee (Fernie and Grant 2019). One newspaper report described further subcontracting services, where unemployed mothers at home during the day with young children, and with encouragement from the job centres, could collect from Doddle on behalf of their neighbours, who would then pick up their parcels on their way home from work. Mothers reportedly earned 50p per parcel. Rossiter also explains how this new workforce of drivers and warehouse workers finds itself displaced geographically to the edge or periphery of the city spaces where the fulfilment and distribution centres are located (Rossiter 2014). Many people from retail who are looking for work will find these jobs unviable. There is both the loss of social contact with customers, and the loss of identity as someone 'working in fashion'. We could say this *e-commerce milieu of fashion labour* marks a further step in the degradation of labour for those working at lower skill levels. For decades, working one's way up to be a store manager for Gap or for Whistles, especially for young people leaving school and not going to university, was a job that carried status and pride. These jobs are now disappearing. This shift also inverts the working lives of the service class, for whom living in close proximity to the city centre enabled at least shorter and cheaper journeys to work (Sassen 1991). Already underpaid and living in inadequate public housing, as well as typically working antisocial hours, these changes simply exacerbate the contingencies of the precarious labour markets for low-qualified, usually disadvantaged people. Where working behind the counter in a well-known department store might in the past have provided an aspirational ladder in what Sassen (2002) labels 'urban glamour zones', this is now a dramatically reduced ambition. Those jobs that do become available are in male-dominated sectors such as warehousing and delivery, or at computer terminals in ports or transport depots. More women are now doing these jobs, but the skill set is quite different from a career in fashion retail.

This recalibration of fashion labour is reflected in a variety of other locations, including what has been referred to as 'listing labour' (Kneese and Palm 2020). This is now required across all areas of fashion retail. From small shops and boutiques to the vintage and second-hand sector, as well as for small-scale fashion designers themselves, it has become necessary to operate an e-commerce system. Large companies can afford to subcontract to digital companies to do this work, but small shops generally do this in-house. Jennifer Ayres (2021) writes about the unpaid labour that is now routinely expected of fashion retail staff that involves posting items online and undertaking various tasks alongside their jobs behind the counter. One of Ayres's respondents described posting items for online sales while on the bus home from work. Others were pressured by store managers to be busy posting when not actually serving customers. Focusing on second-hand and vintage fashion online stores, Tamara Kneese and Michael Palm (2020) document the time-consuming labour involved in the work of listing, from accurate descriptions of the silk blouse or the satin trousers to where the zip is positioned and how the buttons and fastenings work; and then there is the time spent on careful packaging for delicate items, alongside the management of payment systems and, finally, the friendly requests to consumers for good reviews. This amounts to a significant intensification of labour. For small or independent outlets, there are also the piles of returns that have to be processed, parcels opened, inventories adjusted, items checked, washed or freshened and prepared for re-posting online. Big companies have introduced many more customer service resources, such as easy returns, in their bids to remain competitive. Fernie and Grant (2019) provide a full description of the elaborate system of subcontracting returns provided by the Clipper company, which gathers returns for ASOS in a hangar-like German warehouse and then brings those in good enough condition back to the UK to another vast warehouse near the Barnsley ASOS base, where they are prepared for being sent back to the inventory. Reflecting also on the economic power of the fast fashion companies, these authors describe one e-fashion retailer that only charges customers for their purchases once any returns have arrived back at the warehouse and have been processed as such. This operation was testing out the idea that a customer will maybe order five items and return four of them.

There is then a huge expansion in the ranks of fashiontech labour, in computing IT and digital engineering, but also in low-skill areas such as packing and delivery.[8] This new labour force extends to the redesign of so-called 'bricks and mortar' stores so that they are more aligned with not just online shopping, but also with the social media effect of 'mediatization' (Rocamora 2017). This refers to fashion's new hypervisibility not so much through day-to-day social encounters, or as street fashion, but with Instagram self-posting fashion culture. We might, for example, ask what kind of companies install the virtual systems that transform major retail outlets like Burberry's HQ in London's Mayfair into an immersive experience? 'Mediatization' could be understood as contributing a new dimension to the *e-commerce milieu of labour* insofar as it acquires a new directive function. It is not only shops that have to be adjusted to match the online experiences; also, as Agnès Rocamora (2017) suggests, designers must adjust to take into account that clothes will be chosen according to this Instagram criteria, alongside all the other factors. Social media is now an organizational factor, a key part of the *e-commerce milieu of fashion labour* from which many new economic activities proliferate. Fashion is simultaneously devolved and widely spread, with many more actors at every level, and at the same time it expands its reach by breaking down the stable relations that previously existed between producers and consumers. A young woman posting her own collection of fashion items for re-sale, or listing them on Depop, can now describe herself as 'working in fashion'. And so the labour market is totally shaken up. Brands have always chased youth with all kinds of strategies. Huge companies like Depop and Vinted must present themselves in environmentally friendly ways to maintain their popularity with climate-conscious young people. At the same time, fast fashion online companies such as Boohoo sidestep environmental ethics with appeals instead to the pocket-money budgets of teenagers. The whole political economy of fashion is therefore shaken and inconsistency is a noticeable phenomenon. The new strategies for an Italian fashion label are described by a chief digital officer:[9]

> Brands now have multiple channels, and the public have infinite sources of information and inspiration. Once, five photos distributed to the monthly fashion magazine was enough for an average advertising campaign. Today, people follow fashion digital sources that launch offers each day. Brands need to keep attracting attention, so they must spread news each day ... Digital media bring traffic to the shops. We have a meeting every Monday, in which the website and social media people meet with retail and design to coordinate and share information about new arrivals in the shops and online for sale, which products are given to bloggers for their reviews, which photos for the placements, which content needs to be created. I am talking of a fashion brand becoming a sort of a publisher. Today the fashion brand is a newspaper.

Designers in multimediated fashion worlds

If the global pandemic of 2020–22 sealed the fate of the fashion *milieu of labour* to become inextricably tied with e-commerce and the 'mediatization' effect, in what looks to be an irreversible way, the way in which this impacts on the independent sector remains an unfolding phenomenon (at the time of writing in 2021–22). Prior to the Covid-19 pandemic, the designers who were part of the CREATe project had already been scrambling to move to online sales from around 2015–16. This was the point at which having a professional online e-commerce presence became imperative, and it played out for them all according, once again, to the logic of space and the availability of support, from the state, or local government or family and friends. The costs and the labour time involved in moving to a more fully online service were substantial. And even though the work of installing and constantly updating the website became standard and a recognized cost, for microenterprises the further costs on running a sales operation with payment systems became, especially around the question of returns, more challenging. The work involved in posting and packaging and then preparing the returned items to be put back on the rail and re-photographed has become part of the everyday activities of all fashion designers. For those with a shop, the work can be integrated into the usual retail activity, but, as is the case in London, where many designers only have a small studio, the division of labour is less clear and the designer him or herself may well undertake these tasks.

In London each of the four prize-winning designers who took part in the CREATe study had, until the pandemic hit, a fairly straightforward strategy for managing an online presence. Carlo Volpi sold to the edgy subcultural and avant-garde lifestyle shop Darkroom, in Lamb's Conduit Street, and combined this with selling from his own website. But Darkroom closed its doors in 2016 due to rent rises to become an own-brand online retailer with occasional pop-ups and residencies, so that sales outlet for Volpi's swirling giant knits disappeared. More recently, he has been taken up by Not Just A Label (see below) and he has had a long-lasting relationship with Wolf & Badger.[10] During the two years of Covid lockdowns, Volpi focused on teaching and on developing further his collaboration with a Hong Kong woollen company. Teija Eilola sells directly from her own website as well as on Farfetch and she also sells from the Young British Designers site, which was set up in 2010 to specialize in featuring the work of a selective group of UK-based designers. Bruno Basso and Chris Brooke, as mentioned in Chapter 2, decided to take a break from their production schedule just before and then during the pandemic; at the time of writing, their pieces are described as collectibles on both Vestiaire Collective and eBay.

A slight hesitation in Berlin round about 2015 was predicated on the availability of shop and studio space, which, as discussed in Chapter 3, anchored the range of activities for designers in the city, giving them a strong neighbourhood connection. Designers by and large could realistically aim to have their own shops and thus have direct access to customers from friends and community to others across the city, and to tourists. The connection with neighbourhood also obviated the need to rush to move online, especially when the shop could also function as a social space and place for events and gatherings. The designers had invested a good deal of time and energy in this shop-related activity, in the case of Hien Le also moving into a lifestyle concept store. Working on a shoestring and very much part of the long hours culture, the need to then move to e-commerce was not entirely welcome. But, with the pandemic, it became a necessity. It took Esther Perbandt until 2019 to have a fully online sales system in place. By 2021, she had shifted gear into a fully operational online shopping system and she also expanded her range of items with a large jewellery collection. There has been a new emphasis from shop to online with a much more sophisticated website presence than in the past.[11] The lockdown, and the support received from the German government during this period, gave Perbandt the time to reflect on how she could produce more items with cheaper ranges of 'rock star'-type t-shirts and with her hallmark punk-style jewellery. Michael Sontag also prioritized his shop and then decided to work on a bespoke or made-to-order basis (as discussed in Chapter 3). During the pandemic, he too developed a stronger online presence. He introduced a younger look with a street-style gender-neutral sensuality. The models currently wearing his clothes are more diverse than before, and the whole aesthetic is socially engaged and energetic. Both he and Esther Perbandt (two of the key Berlin fashion names) have clearly utilized all the support they have been able to muster to make the move onto a fully online presence with more effective pricings and pay systems. Arguably, they were able to do this during the pandemic because of the lump sum they received for the period of lockdown, and because the loss of regular income during this time did not mean they risked eviction from home or studio. The pandemic also encouraged them to think in more depth about who their audience, consumers, viewers or followers are and have been. As one of the CREATe consultants said: 'With the pandemic, the Berlin designers have tried to involve the customers more. They had to do this. They have been rethinking on the longer term their relationship with customers, and with how they can communicate more directly.'[12] Rita in Palma in Berlin had been selling online as an accessory retailer and designer (as well as a social entrepreneur) for many years. The web presence for Rita in Palma has been distinctive and aimed at growing a strong personalized customer base from the start. Because the owner and founder Ann-Kathrin Carstensen is not herself an *auteur*, she was more easily able to give her time to developing these PR skills and an e-commerce model more rapidly. The brand also features in Haus Glanz, the Berlin based high-end online magazine shop (which specializes in Made in Germany collections and lifestyle goods).

Ajax, Birdsong and Not Just A Label

The opportunities to look at how fast fashion companies develop distinctive labour processes for the new times of fashion-tech came to the CREATe project through the network sociality of the creative clusters in and around Milan. In neither London nor Berlin did it prove possible in the timescale to interview employees of companies such as ASOS or Zalando. But in Milan, because it is a fashion city, where there has long been a surplus of graduates in the creative arts who are constantly looking for work, it was not so hard to be put in touch with three current employees with the proviso of anonymity. The same sense of psycho-logical relief to be working in the new digital fashion economy as we found among others in the Milan scene was apparent for the interviewees who had found work with Ajax. Given that we had already perceived widespread states of depression and anxiety among young graduates in fashion and related fields in Milan, these new opportunities were greeted with high levels of enthusiasm, even euphoria, and a willingness to put in long hours. Our respondents, Tiziana, Maria-Rosa and Loredana, were keen to discuss their jobs. They had quickly assumed a strong identification with the company:

> Packaging is very important. Our packaging is made by a cooperative that employs mostly women. When they have to do parcels for a top brand, they take fifteen minutes each one ... For lower brands they spend less time. Oh, and all our boxes are ecofriendly! ... E-commerce is growing a lot: after all, you spend less, you can try it on at home, and send it back and have a full refund if you don't like it! With the newsletter we keep our costumers up to date, we design ad hoc offers, we try to offer a very customized service. I think customization is key!' (Tiziana)

Maria-Rosa was equally upbeat, as well as keen to describe in even more detail the nature of the job:

> I am an analyst in the purchasing department. My department deals with the planning of the purchases for the season and determines the prices. Ajax is not a fashion enterprise, we market ourselves in these terms because it is a good branding strategy, but in fact it is a tech enterprise. I see e-commerce as an evolution of the traditional shop. But thanks to the e-commerce this shop has global visibility. So, for every brand, besides the retail aspect, the e-commerce window gives the opportunity to showcase the products worldwide. One can think of the rural areas of Italy, or other countries ... before the internet people could have not seen and purchased a lot of products. Their choice was limited to the actual shops in their town.

The third young woman, Loredana, explained how the company worked:

> Ajax has three core businesses: first there is the commercial, the tech aspect, and logistics – it dispatches all over the world in four days for a very low cost, sometimes even for free. This

gives you the idea of the power of the logistics. Everything is dispatched from a single city location in Northern Italy. Second is the service to the brands that use our e-commerce platform, and again logistics is very important. Then third the Ajax storage is totally automatic ... We get like three, four orders per second.

Maria Rosa went on to describe the youthful working culture inside the company. This delivered the kind of excitement associated with Silicon Valley companies in the early days of the internet. It made the workplace particularly appealing, since the young staff appeared to have more decision-making powers than would be the case in other work environments. She was particularly impressed by the algorithmic operations that she claimed were able to adjust a price once they see a is customer online but hesitant about buying. As she said: 'The database and the algorithms do everything, they are fundamental for e-commerce. If you think of all the information, all the sales, campaigns, we have billions of algorithms ... The algorithm converts all the inputs into a desired outcome.'

And Tiziana described the day-to-day working culture. She took only four days holiday in the first year and often worked late, to 8 p.m., knowing that she was not being paid for this overtime:

But yet I am very happy ... every time I go back home thinking I should find another job, 'cos you know ... you feel exploited, but then there is the adrenaline, and when I think of not going in that office I get anxious ... I prefer to have more responsibilities and less money ... I do it for passion ... and my bosses can tell it.

So there was a kind of compromise situation in this fashion new economy workplace. The excitement and the seeming responsibility and flat hierarchies compensated for the low pay. And, compared to most Milanese employers, this company was a beacon of progressive management. Tiziana made this point clearly:

E-commerce is very democratic, very pragmatic, it is a world that tests you all the time. You learn a lot by doing. A colleague of mine has not got a degree but has been working here for ten years ... You learn by doing, it is not something you study ...

Of the people I worked with no one has been sacked ... even if you are not good at what you are doing they are likely to change your tasks, your department ... if you go to the management with a proposal they try to re-assign you.

In the exceptional circumstances of graduate unemployment and people's dependence on the family well into their twenties and even thirties, there is, as we have already noted in Chapter 4, a high degree of middle-class angst about the future, including the future of work. The fashion-tech company is described as a good employer, able to generate an atmosphere even though overtime hours are unpaid. The loyalty, euphoria and feel-good factor reflect the buzz mentality of working for companies like Google and Facebook, and the youth culture ethos is brought to bear in Milan. However, the 'modest' wages suggest that there is no seismic structural change in everyday life – apart from the psychological bonus or improved mental health – from not just having a job, but being able to present oneself in social situations as being part of the internet economy. Fashion-tech in this scenario operates an *e-commerce milieu of labour* that creates jobs, but because these young people do not have professional-level salaries, or indeed overtime pay, the family remains the key site for social reproduction as they gravitate towards this sector of fashion work.

Sophie Slater is the co-founder, along with Sarah Beckett, of the feminist ethical social enterprise online-only label Birdsong, which is based in London and bears the slogan, 'We create clothing for women who dress in protest'. Birdsong is a charity with the aim of bringing a feminist ethos to bear on every part of the company's activities. Initially, when they started in 2014 with a background in fashion retail and women's organizations, what Slater and Beckett were doing was of little interest to the fashion scene in London or, indeed, the UK. At the time, there was little support for a fashion company that emphasized the importance of fair wages for the workforce, that was committed to ensuring the supply chain was not exploitative of employees, that strove to ensure an ethos that did not elevate bodily norms of slimness at the expense of the wide range of body types, that pledged to embrace high levels of environmental awareness and to eliminate wastage and excessive use of plastics. But within three years, things had changed as the politics of fashion came to occupy a much more prominent position. The London-based campaigning organization Fashion Revolution, founded by Orsola de Castro in 2016, was able to mobilize a lot of support from some well-known figures, and the wider forces of climate change activists and young feminists shifted the ground for fashion politics and challenged complacency on the part of the brands. The activism took place primarily on social media and the fact that Birdsong was operating as an online-only retailer fed into the idea that fashion companies could function while also adhering to a social justice agenda. Joined by designer Susanna Wen, Slater and Beckett looked not to the British Fashion Council or its offshoots, but to the not-for-profit and charity sectors, applying for support through schemes for young women entrepreneurs. They also crowdfunded to £100,000. It was a hand-to-mouth existence, as Sophie reported to a group of Goldsmiths students, describing her time 'sofa-surfing' because coming down to London from Yorkshire she could not afford rent.[13] Eventually, she found a workshop space for Birdsong at Euston via the social enterprise projects in London. Birdsong has since garnered a lot of praise and media attention, from the *Guardian*, to *Grazia* magazine, to the *Daily Telegraph* and BBC Radio 4's *Woman's Hour*. The company has been able to expand to support a number of freelancers and makers working in its production centre, all of whom are paid the London living wage.

Fronting the company as a feminist campaigner, Slater has taken part in many panel debates and conferences, especially where the new wave of feminism has connected with environmental issues and with combating racism. Her newsletter also carries regular features that cultivate and engage with followers/readers/customers, who are updated on new projects and on the steps being taken to ensure that Birdsong fulfils its social justice agenda. Throughout the pandemic, the company adjusted its stock to reflect the working-from-home situation, while also preparing new elements, including a packaging and delivery centre in a former factory in Kentish Town, North London, which employs people from the disabled community with pay being fully compliant with the London living wage. (The website features a YouTube video showing this workforce at the packing tables.) Fashion social justice underpins the Birdsong work, but social media in effect holds the concept together. The team posts on Twitter, Facebook and Instagram on an almost daily basis. Equal attention is given to the new items in the collection and the wider social issues connecting to the fashion scene. These range from challenging dominant ideals of thinness, to not just featuring black models in the images, but also ensuring ethnic minority participation at every level of the undertaking. Slater has become a leading campaigning figure in the new world of fashion politics in the UK in the space of seven years, including during the pandemic and its aftermath.[14] Birdsong has shown that there are other ways of doing fashion and there is a model here that could be rolled out in other towns and cities. She has shown that an online company can galvanize a local workforce, and this produces new forms of job creation in a social justice environment. However, there are considerable challenges in financing this model of doing fashion differently. The very fact of its survival and success in London reflects the exceptional levels of commitment to the project by the directors, since the company is not part of the high fashion scene and is not going to attract sponsorship from the glossy brands and so relies on its social media presence for sales and for communicating its values.

Like Birdsong, Not Just A Label (NJAL) is an online-only fashion business that offers a made-to-order service, with customers receiving the goods within three weeks of placing the order. NJAL specializes in high-end luxury independent designers from across the world, whose work can be purchased through the company's webpages.[15] There is also a newspaper/ newsletter format, with journalists and others often providing feature-type articles.[16] The owner, Stefan Siegel, was very much a pioneer of fashion-tech when he set up the company in 2008. He was well placed to do this given his background in economics and finance and time also spent in media and advertising. His knowledge of the industry (having grown up in a family with fashion connections in northern Italy), made possible the entry into the idea of fashion-tech as well as access to venture capital. He started with an office in Shoreditch, London, then, when rents rose, he swiftly moved to the new fashion and creative hubs of Los Angeles; more recently, he once again has an office in London's luxury fashion location of the Dover Street Market. The scale of the undertaking is remarkable in that up to 45,000 designers have shown their work in a portfolio format on the site. The emphasis is on newcomers and up-and-coming names from across the world.[17] NJAL sees itself as providing a service function supporting independent design. The online format means that designers can showcase their work and be seen without having gone through the filter process of the London-based (or New York-based) art and design schools. So this model actually decentralizes the capital city effect, while showcasing designers whose work might otherwise not get seen by other fashion professionals. As Siegel said:

> I decided to go into the corporate side and worked for Ernst and Young and then Merrill Lynch on the investment banking side, but always in fashion. So I saw the fashion industry from the investment side and I think that's where the idea [for NJAL] came up. It was hard for us to find designers or brands to invest in. And then speaking to schools like Central Saint Martins, they didn't have an alumni network, I always thought that that is what business schools are really good at, creating networks, clubs and websites where you can find jobs. I thought no one has really done that in fashion where it could be so valuable. Me and my brother built up the first test – an open-source platform that allowed designers to show their work in a different way. They were all using Myspace back then, and we felt like that wasn't professional enough. That's how we launched ... We wanted to create a way where we can give them the basic support, that in the first instance was digital. Most designers back then didn't have a website. So we were the first website for most of these designers ... For us it is about empowering small artisans, connecting people locally, selling globally, doing things in a completely different way. We change the whole system, we don't pay rent, and so automatically the designer gets a bigger share of what NJAL sells. (Interview, 2016)

Siegel's model is closer to a full-scale scout-for-talent corporate undertaking, with funds coming from the consultancy wing of his business as well as some investment from Vivienne Westwood. NJAL presents and curates the designers on the site. It is a big undertaking: the online global shop window offers a huge choice of original, adventurous but also quite mainstream collections.[18] In common with large fashion-tech companies, the actual business model remains quite nebulous. The promise is the ability to bring new designers from across the world who would otherwise not get this kind of window to show work because they do not have the credentials of graduates from the London or New York schools. Siegel is able to showcase this talent and to arrange introductions to the big brands on the basis of his networking and portfolio consultancy work. But at ground level, NJAL is a service and platform provider offering advice and support, including an enhanced package to include software updates to create more professional online presence and to bring designers more fully up to date. As an increasingly well-known presence in the fashion-tech world, NJAL seems poised to accrue value on the futures market, while at the same time functioning as a portal to present global fashion newcomers in the e-retail format. Siegel is a platform fashion intermediary, talent-scouting, networking globally and able to connect with the financial big players on the futures market.

Conclusion

Having identified e-commerce as the emerging dominant *milieu of fashion labour*, there remains the question of how platform fashion-tech exerts its power with regard to weaker players and independents in each of the three cities that figure in this study. As capitalism's most recent mode of production, e-commerce is not just software and engineering, infrastructure and logistics; it is also fierce competition, losses, buy-outs, take-overs and mergers, where the stakes are so high and alongside which is the constant aim of driving costs down, especially labour costs, hence the 'degradation of labour'. A lasting tension exposed in this book is the relation between the big, all-powerful brands and the small independents. E-commerce and the big brands exist in a different economic space from local government and the art and design schools that have been pinpointed earlier on as important *milieus of fashion labour*, especially in London and Berlin. Finance capital exerts a good deal of control over what local councils are able to do, by means of loans and debt management. The joint impact of fashion-tech and finance capital creates new jobs, many of which are at the low end of the skill range. Multiple factors must therefore be taken into account when the fashion industry is viewed through this optic of e-commerce. What will happen to the now empty shops dotted along high streets from small towns to capital cities? Has the pandemic accelerated their permanent closure? If this is the case, will the property market hollow out and space suddenly become affordable for the kinds of designers and other creatives who have been priced out of London? Or will the companies that own these spaces leave them empty and sit it out for a few years until the economy, especially the financial economy, is rebooted? As we write, in May 2022, all the signs are that London rents are once again rising (Cox 2022). Can the 'monopoly rent' of London be broken or dented by a combination of fashion-tech and the processes of relocalization that the pandemic inaugurated? Meanwhile, e-commerce wrecks its own new environmental havoc as city streets are clogged up with vans and trucks day and night making home deliveries. There is no shortage of turmoil and disruption, and the fashion-tech sector finds itself reliant on huge flows of investment, mostly from China, to maintain liquidity. Fashion-tech also looks to China for new markets where there is less vocal radical campaigning and fewer organized protests against the fashion industry. Alibaba has helped Farfetch to expand its operations, while at the same time being exposed for its own poor labour practices that rely on what Beijing insiders call the 9:9:6 system – i.e., working from 9 a.m. to 9 p.m. six days a week, as reported by the UK *Financial Times*.[19] In short, fashion-tech, despite the lack of profits, is buoyed up by a business confidence that relies on the futures market while its CEOs are already so personally wealthy that their own futures, should the enterprises fail, are not in doubt. Social polarization and wealth inequality are constantly created in fashion culture today. In the absence of a social wage underpinning and supporting young designers in the UK, even when they are able to function online as independent e-retailers, they face many hurdles for their own daily lives and social reproduction. They need studio space, and a shop front is still important even with a strong online presence and capacity. But space remains prohibitively expensive.

To sum up, this chapter has shown the emergence of fashion-tech as a platform-based *milieu of labour*. This reconfigures, without supplanting, the previous *milieus of labour*. They must now all sit alongside each other. There is indeed the potential for a more decentralized regional fashion culture to emerge, which could nurture local and neighbourhood consumers, while also using fashion-tech to produce for more people far and wide. This kind of radical model for fashion production would also enable many more actors to enter the field, especially those who have been marginalized. No longer would young people have to head to exorbitantly expensive cities like London in order to pursue a career in fashion; they could remain at home in Liverpool or Aberdeen creating hybrid modes of production. This kind of pathway enabled by fashion-tech could also definitively break the grip of the big brands and fast fashion. In all three of our chosen locations for this study, this potential exists, but in each case there would need to be a group of deter-mined fashion cultural intermediaries willing to play a role as new kinds of policymakers, knocking on the doors of town halls, arguing on grounds of gender and racial equality in the sector and on grounds of a greener fashion future. Such initiatives as these would also need to be able to grapple with the power of the big brands and their adeptness at returning to a fashion status quo even when faced with challenges such as the pandemic and the increasingly loud voices of the new fashion radicals.

6
Conclusion

The fashion industry is at a crossroads. The degree of turmoil and uncertainty and the calls for moral account-ability are unprecedented. This is an unexpected situation and very different from what was in place at the outset of our study. Although our lens was more narrowly set on the idea of the microenterprise in the three cities we decided to investigate, having a sociological perspective throughout meant that we were constantly looking beyond the frame of the designer's day-to-day working lives to reflect on wider precarity in the creative industries. We were also alert to ideas of generational consciousness and to the dynamics of social change, especially those accruing from the rapid escalation of property prices in the UK and the way this has dominated how people live and work. Anti-gentrification struggles have become a regular occurrence in all three cities that featured in this study. Equally important has been the tidal wave of opposition to the environmentally toxic practices that have long characterized fashion per se. The forcefulness of the critique of fashion has grown louder and has expanded to include many more interconnected issues in recent years. And the new radical voices are coming from many different angles. Organizations like Fashion Revolution have found wide support in the struggle to push the whole industry towards adhering to a green agenda from top to bottom, from the agricultural level up through to textile production, and from there to the chemical and dyeing industry, to waste management, land refill systems, to the damage wrought by fast fashion and throwaway culture, to debates about modern-day slavery, supply chains and exploitative and unhealthy working conditions found in the world's low-pay and cheap labour factories. Hundreds of campaigning groups have sprung into life with a loud presence on social media, such as Clean Clothes Campaign, Centre for Sustainable Fashion, Labour Behind the Label, ReMake, TRAID, Fashion for Good, and many others. This new activism, spearheaded by young people, was never at the forefront of this current study, yet its influence and its vocal presence in the classrooms and seminars, as well as in so much news coverage, has in many ways bolstered our confidence to make the case for fashion to be even more socially engaged and for it to become less of a hierarchical glamour industry and more of a popular aesthetic of everyday life, which also has the ability to create meaningful jobs for people in non-exploitative environments. A 'social fashion' system could bring its benefits and its pleasures to a wider range of people, by establishing fashion hubs and production centres in various towns and cities across the UK, not just in London and the South-East. (And likewise in cities across the other two countries we have considered – Germany and Italy.) This point is particularly salient because of the broad range of excellent universities with long established fashion and textiles departments. Instead of dispatching their students to the London's 'transaction-rich agglomeration' of fashion centres, there could be a range of incentives for graduates in Aberdeen, or in Cardiff, to stay put or to find fashion jobs in other nearby towns and cities across the length and breadth of the UK (Scott 2000). The egalitarian effect here would be in the spread of new jobs and the better access opportunities for working-class and ethnic minority people, especially those with family responsibilities.

Feminism has also had an important role to play in our study, and this too has been a topic that has recently reverberated more widely across the fashion industry. This is a new feminism, which has developed a sexual politics of fashion highlighting racism and abusive practices within and across sectors, from the sexual harassment of models to the exploitation of women in the sweatshops conditions of many manufacturers across the world. Alongside this has been the attack on sexual and racial stereotyping and the bodily normativity that has excluded many women while also fuelling harmful eating disorders and epidemic-level patterns of low self-esteem and self-loathing among teenage girls. Voices from the LGBTQ and queer communities have urged designers to refuse the gender normativity of fashion. The editor of British *Vogue*, Edward Enninful, has emphasized that black people need to be employed in the fashion-related creative industries more widely, as talent behind the scenes and also in journalism and writing. Across this study we found significant underrepresentation of black and ethnic minority independent designers, which is especially shocking in a multicultural city like London. The two black women designers who joined the study were both directly linked with Goldsmiths, one on the faculty and both having completed their PhDs in the institution.

In 2022, the scope for developing policies that could deliver a truly 'social fashion' system needs more detailed fleshing out. The sociology of activism and protest movements is, by now, an advanced field of study, but so far this kind of attention has not been directed towards charting the many fashion campaigns, their social media and other strategies, their impact and their overarching political philosophy. Academic fashion industry research has always been stymied by the difficulties of gaining access to the big brands and the leading institutions. However, opening their doors to keen young sociologists and anthropologists could be beneficial to these companies too. It has rarely if ever happened. At the very least it would show them to be modern and open-minded rather than wrapped in secrecy and mystique. Likewise, it would be important to develop a clearer picture of the policymaking bodies, their remit and their reach into relevant government departments and local authorities and regional bodies. So far, we have mentioned activist sites and environmental campaigning organizations such as Fashion Revolution. The Fashion Roundtable think-tank has only recently been established, but with a strong policy agenda and lines of connection to government through facilities such as the all-party parliamentary groups, it has emerged as the voice most likely to be listened to at the national level.

No one could have dreamt of a pandemic as catastrophic as that which spread across the world in 2020. This has reverberations in many still unknown ways across the creative sector. There is an urgency now for researchers to document the full impact of the pandemic and how it may also have encouraged a new mindset in the creative economy for the better (Banks 2020). Likewise, when this current research for CREATe began in 2014–15, although the possibility of a Brexit outcome existed, it was not until the days following the result in 2016 that the reality began to sink in and people became aware of the extent to which things would change, not least in the European university research culture. There was then a period of time during which new legislation was being drafted. In the university and art school sector, the decision that EU students were to be charged full international fees from 2021 was not announced until 2020. This ruling makes it difficult for anyone other than students from wealthy families to come to the UK to study for a Master's, as many of our respondents had done in the previous years. This is arguably catastrophic for the lively cosmopolitan culture that has been fostered in UK universities in recent years. For the independent art school-trained designers, Brexit and the pandemic have together had massively detrimental impacts on their ability to develop and expand their studio practice. A recent report points out that 'pre-Brexit the EU accounted for 80% of the sector's exports and 30% of fashion imports'; the 'fear of rising costs, delays, border checks and increasing administration' amounts to a major challenge (Harris et al. 2021: 23). The new situation has repercussions at every point in the design cycle. The past ease with which someone like Teija Eilola (see Chapter 2) dealt with her French agent and the various shops and boutiques in France has been replaced by a much more onerous and perhaps impossible to sustain business model. It is only now, in 2022, that issues about skills shortages post-Brexit have become a major news item, but this is already another blow for fashion, interrupting both the reliance on EU nationals living and working in the UK and with the right skills for the fashion sector, but more substantially for EU

workers in East European factories, which have long been
the favoured site for independent fashion production for the
UK. In May 2021, the Fashion Roundtable drew attention
to the whole gamut of problems that have been exacerbated
by Brexit, from exports to skills shortages, to the need
for fast turnaround visas for UK models to do the kind of
work they would have done in Paris at short notice. Many
companies, it seems, have considered relocating to get round
the enormous difficulties posed by the UK now having to
prove place of origin of items that have been part-produced
outside the UK and only finished inside the UK. The time and
costs involved mean that the bigger companies can afford to
consider setting up distribution centres in an EU country,
but not the small start-ups and microenterprises. Alongside
delays in deliveries, problems with movement of goods and
services, skill shortages, especially for machinists, costs to
reputation and problems accessing new customers, there
are now mountains of paperwork and many obstacles that
comprise a major disincentive. This will surely put even more
pressure on the kinds of independent labels that the UK has
been known for across the world. For established companies
it means the need for high-level lobbying and campaigning
that draw on well-known figures from across the sector.
Letters to government signed by hundreds make the point
that fashion is as deserving as the fishing industry, which
received a £23 million package. The Fashion Roundtable
report also highlights the impact on freelance workers in
fashion who, like musicians, have been used, prior to Brexit,
to travelling across EU countries for work at short notice up
to forty times per year and who now find a new system in
place that means it can take three months to secure a visa.
This flow of talent has been a key characteristic of fashion
labour, with UK freelance designers often supporting their
own labels by working for a few weeks at a time for more
mainstream high-street European brands. In this context,
there are, not surprisingly, urgent calls for visa waivers for
creative workers, new 'bilateral agreements' between the UK
and the EU to ease the pain inflicted on the sector, and even
the introduction of a 'cabotage' system, which would entail
full exemptions for the fashion industry. The think-tank
Fashion Roundtable is now a vital force for representing the

sector. Their 2021 report described a scenario of deepening crisis, as job opportunities in EU countries dry up, or simply become unviable for independent and self-employed highly qualified designers based in the UK. Microenterprises will also be affected by the shortages of skilled machinists from EU countries, since their projected annual wages do not meet the current threshold for visa applications. (Hence the Fashion Roundtable rightly makes the case for wages to rise to fit this requirement as a matter of social justice, and for fair wages in the sector.)

We end this book by picking up some themes addressed in another recent project led by Sandy Black and Dilys Williams, titled Fostering Sustainable Practices (2021). Case studies of the small-scale fashion enterprises that feature in this thirty-month project demonstrate a dynamic commitment to 'changing the mindset'. Several of the designers describe how far from the idea of the conventional business model their own practices have moved. There is a critique of the ideas of profit and constant growth. Many have diversified to work with galleries and museums. Across the whole cohort, addressing the climate crisis drives their design practice and this in turn means constantly reviewing the place of fashion in the wider ecosystem. Community engagement comes forward, including working with disadvantaged groups such as women who have been through the criminal justice system. Transforming fashion into a rewarding place of work with fair pay, flat hierarchies and skill-sharing all point to the scale of the shift. These microenterprises all answer the question: how is it possible to do fashion in an entirely different way? Reports from the FSP work from March 2021 are heartening and also supportive of the kinds of claims we have made in the course of this book. This pushes us to take our parallel line of inquiry even further and propose that the 'social fashion' model and the not-for-profit ethos that underscore the social enterprises we found on the ground in the Berlin neighbourhoods can be extended to reconfigure the normative social relationships that underpin the mainstream fashion system. Perhaps the language of product, market and customers or consumers can be replaced with a different vocabulary. This prompts us to suggest that the logic of social fashion would also extend to the way we describe

the materiality of the objects that are produced, and those
who buy them. We could think in future about how the
works, the items or the pieces appeal to different groups of
people. We could understand this as a relational economy
where designers, like artists, show their work, encourage
buyers, keep in touch with their audiences and provide some
wider cultural experiences for their readers and viewers or
the followers of websites who, in turn, are willing to spend
some money for the pieces. Many of our participants have
already been doing this over the years – we need only think
of the *dérive* socks from Kenneth Mackenzie or the crochet
socks from Rita in Palma, or the rock-star performances of
Esther Perbandt. These wider cultural practices demonstrate
not only the emphasis on the aesthetics of value, but also the
promise that fashion has a vital role to play in the politics and
pleasures of everyday life.

Appendix

Throughout this study, we adhered to all the standard ethical guidelines for qualitative research. Since the research was undertaken over a substantial period of time, and involved so many different activities and events, some of which involved the respondents and interviewees, as fashion professionals, themselves giving talks and speeches, we have referred in the text primarily to interviews and to email correspondences. On a few occasions, we refer to comments made in the course of a talk. The following people all played a role in the research for CREATe AHRC 2013–18, and of course we wish to thank them all warmly.

Berlin

Issever Bahri
Clara Brandenburg
Alexander Brett
Ann-Kathrin Carstensen (Rita in Palma)
Stefan Dietzelt (The Director's Cut)
Melissa Drier (WWD)
Maria Exner (Zeit online)
Daniela Fleig (NEMONA)
Anne Frank (Majaco)

Marte Hentschel (Sqetch)
Ares Kalandides
Bastian Lange (Multiplicities)
Hien Le
Oliver MacConnell
Tanja Muehlhans (Berlin Senate)
Esther Perbandt
Elke Ritt (British Council)
Michael Sontag
Bettina Springer
Augustin Teboul
Agnes Zelei

London

Bruno Basso and Chris Brooke (Basso and Brooke)
Christine Checinska
Teija Eilola
Sine Fiennes
Dan Henderson
Margaret Howell
Alex Jones
Kenneth Mackenzie (6876)
Tania Phipps-Rufus
Sian Prime
Stefan Siegel (Not Just A Label)
Rose Sinclair
Sophie Slater (Birdsong)
Carlo Volpi

Milan

Adam Arvidsson
Francesca Avian and Erica Agogliati (Flatwig)
Denise Bonapace
Laura Bovone
Francesco Cefalogli
Marianne D'Ovidio
Elisa Fregna and Antonella Bellina (DueDiLatte)

Matthan Gori
Giannino Malossi
Maria Cristina Manzoni
Benedetta Quaratesi
Zoe Romano
Ela Siromancenko (Elochka)
Camilla Vinciguerra (BeConvertible)

Events hosted

October Gallery, Berlin 2012; Goldsmiths, University of London 2014; Goldsmiths, University of London 2015; Berlin Fashion Week 2015; Berlin Fashion Week 2016; British Council, Berlin 2016; Milan University Statale 2016; Glasgow School of Art 2016; CREATe Festival, Glasgow 2016; Royal Society for the Arts 2017; Technische Universität, Berlin 2020; Goldsmiths, University of London 2021.

Methodological note

Our AHRC budget was small over the duration of this project and we were grateful to Goldsmiths, University of London for providing us with further support. With these constraints, our respondents were all recruited through personal and professional contacts and there was some snowballing effect. In the early months, we attempted to make contact with approximately twelve younger UK independent designers, from whom we had either no response or a note back indicating they were too busy.

Notes

Introduction

1 See Fashion Roundtable (2021).
2 In 2021, Berlin's techno DJs put in a bid for UNESCO world heritage status; see Tapper (2021).
3 Defined as coming after the so-called First Italy in the north and north-east, characterized by full-scale industrialization, and in contrast to the Second Italy in the south, which was mostly characterized by uneven small family businesses, the Third Italy developed from the mid-1970s with organized clusters of specialist artisan workshops and craft-based firms connecting with each other on a district model.

Chapter 1: Critical Fashion Studies: Paradigms for Creative Industries Research

1 See Bull (2019); Saha (2019).
2 For a different narrative of this development, one that looks to the terrain of arts and cultural policy, see Oakley and Ward (2018). They date this focus back to 1988 with reference to bodies such as the UK Arts Council.
3 For example, Curran and Hesmondhalgh (2019).
4 Tony Bennet (1992, 1995) at the Open University also contributed to these debates.

5 See also Sean Nixon (1996).

6 However, as Josephine Berry (2015) points out, the comman-
deering of culture, for the sake of responding to the new
postindustrial economy, as a means of beginning a process of
deregulating planning to permit a new regime of financialization
to take root in rundown urban areas, actually dates back to the
early 1980s with the Garden Festivals and the Cities of Culture
overseen by Michael Heseltine. See also interviews by Jonathan
Gross (2020) at King's College London.

7 By paradigm, we mean those dominant existing and systematic
models that have defined the field of research, as distinctive
perspectives, as clear ways of looking.

8 There is an established tradition of object analysis in dress
history. Our aim differs from this approach by considering
the fashion item in more sociological terms as a 'distributional
object', which sets in motion a range of relational activities and
effects for its users or consumers or viewers (Rancière 2008).

9 Fashion is a global supply chain industry. Ideally, we would be
able to trace the genesis of the pieces in a collection through
their production and manufacture stages, and then to the retail
outlet and into the hands of the customer. Sadly, such an undertaking is beyond the scale of this current investigation.

10 Jim McGuigan's (2005) writing on the Dome also blazed this
trail.

11 This new position is expressed in Florida (2017).

12 See Banks and O'Connor (2017) for an account of Manchester's
hopes in the early days for real jobs being created through
local government support and for the uplifting effect that a
'progressive urban cultural economy' promised.

13 For example, with the development of the new Trampery studio
spaces at Fish Island, it is noted that the rents are affordable,
from £300 per months for a well-equipped garage-style space; see
https://www.thetrampery.com/spaces/workspaces/fish-island/.

14 Of course, any such back-tracking also depends on the political
make-up of local councils and the organizational forms of urban
governance. In Berlin since 2018, there has been, in the Senate,
a Red-Red-Green (*Rot-Rot-Grün*) coalition, and this has indeed
prompted a shift away from cultural policies that appear to
actively encourage gentrification.

15 For example, see the British Council Report (2020).

16 For case studies, see the 2017 special issue of *Cultural Sociology*
(vol. 11, issue 3) edited by Dave O'Brien, Kim Allen, Sam
Friedman and Anamik Saha.

17 The Greater London Council (GLC) promoted this provision

under the rubric of dedicated housing associations until it was disbanded by Margaret Thatcher in 1986.

18 The limitations of our own empirical investigations relate to budgets, and to multiple obligations of the team.

19 Details of the rent cap in Berlin are explained by Dullroy (2020). For the repeal of the rent control decisions, see Hall (2021).

20 See figures 1, 2, 3, 4 and 5. The Glasgow School of Art hosted an afternoon event organized as a key part of the CREATe research project. Speakers included a number of the participating designers from London and Berlin, as well as the principal investigator for the AHRC programme Philip Schlesinger and the eminent fashion historian Christopher Breward.

21 The idea of the event was central to the methodology as a way of providing more reciprocity for the designers and others who took part. There were panel discussions in the form of evening seminars, and one-day conferences open to wider audiences in each city, including Glasgow, Scotland. Our respondents were encouraged to present their own ideas and to take part in ongoing discussions as professionals.

22 Hito Steyerl, the German artist and writer, is most often cited in these contexts.

23 This emerges from the sustainable fashion campaigns for re-using and recycling all items of clothing so that they avoid ending up in landfills or being burnt.

24 Born's subsequent work involved ethnography undertaken in music department classrooms at universities and colleges; see Born 2013; Born and Barry 2018.

25 Another designer we interviewed, Alex Jones, had one of his dresses bought and worn by Kylie Minogue, which helped his cashflow over the following months.

26 In her short talk at the Goldsmiths University Fashion Futures event on 31 May 2021, Bethany Williams described her long hours and low income that resulted from setting up her own business. However, she also said how much she loved the work.

Chapter 2: London: Independent Fashion and 'Monopoly Rent'

1 This *Guardian* article continues: 'After the government cut the maintenance grant for hardship and students had to start paying for their higher education via a series of loans, the university experience has been irrevocably altered. It's been a long time

since such big names as J. W. Anderson's founder Jonathan Anderson and Jimmy Choo graduated from the London College of Fashion, UAL.' https://www.theguardian.com/fashion/2016 /jun/06/graduate-fashion-week-why-money-more-than-talent -key-education-british-fashion-council.

2 Note from Angela McRobbie: 'From 1982 to 1985, I was a sessional lecturer in cultural studies at CSM, London. To say the building on Charing Cross Road was in a poor state of repair is an understatement. The concrete and wood staircases and long dark corridors were full of cracks and holes, the student café was airless and windowless, the edit suites for film students were in a cramped basement, there were constant leaks and the ceilings bore the traces of this alongside decrepit toilets. Apart from a few grumbles from the fashion students about not having big enough tables for pattern-cutting in the Greek Street annex round the corner, there were rarely student complaints. With Soho round the corner full of cheap places to eat and any number of pubs, staff and students could carry on with seminars after hours.'

3 In March 2021, Rightmove was advertising 'build to rent' two-bedroom apartments in new King's Cross at an average of £2,200 per month plus council tax. One-bedroom rents averaged £1,500 plus council tax.

4 There have always been difficulties in getting an 'own label' enterprise off the ground for lower-income graduates, especially those from ethnic minorities. Space as well as bank loans and cost of equipment have deterred many from this pathway.

5 To even begin to explore this question, we would need to consider Britain's long history with regard to university places offered to Commonwealth students, and also the rapid expansion of the international student body through processes of globalization from the late 1970s. Coterminous with the imperialistic ambition, however, was the production by the aforesaid students of marvellously effervescent cosmopolitan spaces across the entire UK university system.

6 For a range of rooms and prices of student accommodation in London, see www.unitestudents.com/london.

7 As witnessed during the 2020–22 global pandemic, when students were required to move into their accommodation at a time when all teaching was online and academic staff were working from home. In some cases, the students were virtually incarcerated in their fenced-off halls of residence.

8 Retail became casualized in London from the late 1990s, offering central London fashion jobs in outlets like Gap or

Agnes b primarily for students able to do shift work and who
were flexible with regard to casual and zero hours contracts.
9 The Grenfell Tower disaster resulted in the deaths of sixty-eight
people, mostly low-income families, but included in the death
toll was a young Italian couple, Gloria Trevisan aged 26 and
Marco Gottardi aged 27, who were studying architecture. They
were living at the very top of the tower and prior to the fire
wrote with great enthusiasm to their parents back home about
the views and how they had made their rented flat into a stylish
home.
10 There are further references to investment by an Australian
pension fund with a 25% stake, which is indicative of the
success of the redevelopment programme.
11 This does not however stretch to the social housing remit
providing anything like the overall quality of the private
apartments, as the debate about the so-called 'poor door'
demonstrates – see Osborne (2014).
12 See Moore (2016).
13 The site also hosts London campuses for Loughborough
University and Staffordshire University, with their largely
international student cohorts also being part of the renting
population.
14 See Hitchen and Faz 2021.
15 Early signs of this could be seen in the late 1990s, first on
the Holloway Road from Highbury, Islington, alongside the
University of North London, and stretching up as far as
Archway, including pocket developments in Tufnell Park, but
more visibly connecting to the Caledonian Road through developments along North Road, N7. Similar developments have
appeared in concentrated blocks around Finsbury Park Station,
winding back to Holloway on Iseldon Road.
16 And if students are sources for the extraction of value, there
is a significant deterioration of working conditions for those
who teach them, as colleges and universities increasingly rely
on young academics, who are employed on short-term and
precarious contracts and expected to work long hours over and
above what they are contracted for. Here we see another prime
example of the 'degradation of labour'.
17 Giving rise also to new kinds of jobs, e.g., making assessments
about the kinds of retail that fit with and complement and
extend the value of the existing facilities.
18 London is also being rapidly de-cosmopolitanized as the many
international graduate students who went on to build a professional identity for themselves in the UK, especially in the new

creative field, have found themselves by their mid to late-30s already feeling that it is impossible to plan for a family life in London and the South-East because housing costs are so exorbitant. Many consider returning to their country of origin.

19 Established in 2020, Fashion Roundtable is a think-tank for the sector, with newsletters, events, reports and a range of all-party parliamentary groups (APPGs).

20 See Fostering Sustainable Practices 2021.

21 The websites for both the new development of the Trampery at HWFI and for the existing CFE set out bold plans for supporting young designers so that they can grow and develop the business skills that will see them succeed in the global fashion industry.

22 In recent years, and under the Creative Clusters AHRC initiatives, there has been a shift away from business school vocabulary. Instead, there has been a well-timed set of collaborations between fashion and textile academics at LCF and STEM-based scientists and engineers under the rubric of environmental textile technologies (Harris et al. 2021).

23 The cost of renting has become prohibitive, which stymies the possibility of saving for a deposit. By 2013 Boris Johnson, then Mayor of London, was promising affordable housing with starter homes at £450,000 (Minton 2017).

24 In 2020–21, international fees for Master's at CSM were between £25,800 and £32,900; undergraduate home fees were £11,220.

25 Leftwing London Council under leadership of Ken Livingstone.

26 From the webpages for 6876: '*Dérive* Socks: The concept of the *dérive* has its origins in the Letterist International, an avant-garde and Marxist collective based in Paris. The *dérive* was a critical tool for understanding and developing the theory of psychogeography, defined as the "specific effects of the geographical environment (whether consciously organized or not) on the emotions and behavior of individuals". Guy Debord defines the *dérive* as "a mode of experimental behavior linked to the conditions of urban society".'

27 See Sinclair 2015.

28 During the pandemic, however, the family decided to move permanently to Cornwall and to work remotely from there.

29 Which, as he commented, 'creates a kind of adrenaline high, a euphoria of wanting more'.

30 The Cockpit is a historic studio space established during the more generous years of the GLC. Over creaking wooden floorboards, it houses up to forty crafts-based artists in a rabbit warren of studios stretching over four floors of former

warehouse space. It provides support for its resident craftsmen and women in the form of help in applying for funds to cover the cost of the studio space and for equipment, and most spaces are shared by up to four persons. What's also important about the Cockpit, and is also a hangover from past times, is that it has an equal opportunities agenda, which makes it quite different in atmosphere from the more hipster-style start-up environment of, for example, the Trampery, which, in its first format, charged almost £400 per week for a small cubicle-like work space. Unusually in fashion, the Cockpit considers applications from creative people who have been unemployed or who have been excluded from the more official and competitive routes into the creative economy. In our conversation with one of the directors, she drew attention to those barriers, including the high cost of childcare or having a disability. This vocabulary itself was in marked contrast to those found in the glossy brochures associated with spaces like the CFE and with support from the BFC.

31 During the pandemic the well-known ex-CSM fashion designer Molly Goddard was signed up to create a homeware range for John Lewis.

32 CSM attracts the offspring of various celebrities, such as Madonna and Jude Law more recently, and, in the 1980s, Stella, the daughter of Paul McCartney; see Moore (2015).

Chapter 3: Berlin: Microenterprises and the Social Face of Fashion

1 A report from Berlin Partner GmbH (2005) estimated that there were 'over 800 trend-setting designers and labels at work in the capital'. More recent estimates for designers running their own studios suggest that there are approximately 300.

2 Danielle Fleig, a manager of the social enterprise project NEMONA, described the activities and the funding models at an event hosted by Goldsmiths, University of London at the October Gallery, Kreuzberg, in 2012.

3 In 2000, the Berlin Club Commission set up an organizing body for 189 clubs in the city to be active against displacement caused by gentrification and 'first point of contact in the club scene for cultural policy'. See 'The Club Is Also About Excess': interview on 12 March 2021 by Jens Uthoff with Club Commission chair; https://taz.de/Clubcommission-Vorsitzende-im-Interview/!5754701.

4 A comment made by sociologist Anja Schwanhäuser (2010), who documented the club scene as a specific form of 'Berlin capitalism' during the piloting of this project in 2012.

5 Most recent is 'Neustarthilfe Berlin', an aid package designed to alleviate the impact of the Covid pandemic for the self-employed and small businesses, announced on 23 February 2021. Senate Berlin Department for Economy, Energy and Businesses, press release.

6 To be a subject of entitlement to the benefits system, to access, for example, Arbeitslosgeld, or to be able to apply for support for rent or for a subsidized working space means having the right kind of citizenship status. In addition, the levels of bureaucracy and paperwork require skills and know-how to be able to navigate the welfare state system.

7 Though the pandemic has prompted discussion about how designers can find better ways of communicating with their customers, as well as using social media to attract new followers. This is apparent from the tone and style on Facebook pages and Twitter. It is a point we follow up in Chapter 5.

8 We interviewed the creative director of Jil Sander in Milan where the company has its HQ and is now, in effect, an Italian company, although the actual ownership constantly moves between different private equity companies.

9 Where many would be put to work in labour camps bent over on the same sewing machines to produce glamourous gowns for Nazi wives and girlfriends (Westphal 2020).

10 The image of functional reliability in German fashion echoes through the pages of the Oxford Economics report, 'The Status of German Fashion' (2021).

11 We define *milieu of labour* as in the previous chapters to refer to the capacity-generating agencies issuing from the local or national state, also including in this case those EU programmes for cultural policy and job creation.

12 One of our leading respondents, Marte Hentschel, founder of various fashion producer services, pointedly remarked, after a talk by the UK enterprise culture manager and adviser Sian Prime (also a Goldsmiths colleague and member of the CREATe team), 'but we were brought up on punk and the avant-garde'. This in turn elicited a response from the Senate politician present, Tania Muelhans, in charge of the Office for Women, Economy and Technology. She said that it is precisely the kind of training in business studies and cultural entrepreneurship to which Sian Prime alluded that, in her view, was absolutely needed in Berlin. Some months later, in an interview held at

her workplace in the Schöneberg Rathaus, she voiced her frustration that many of the fashion designers in the city did not have commercial acumen and were instead looking for support and public subsidy. These ongoing research conversations, where events are followed up with interviews, and where our actors engaged in public dialogue with one another, became a key feature of the methodologies over the course of the project. This approach allowed us to see the respondents, in this case designers and policymakers, talking to each other often quite spontaneously. See Born and Barry (2018).

13 See   https://handbookgermany.de/en/work/self-employment .html.

14 For details of how such a project works, see Kalandides (2014).

15 Friedelstr, Lenaustrasse, Hobrechtstrasse, Pflügerstrasse.

16 See, for example, Bernt and Holm (2009) and Jakob (2009). More recently there has been a surge of building in the formerly rundown Friedrichshain with the appearance of a huge WeWork and something called The Student Hotel in the same development.

17 One of our respondents, Hien Le, commented on how coming third in a competition, 'Start Your Own Business', allowed him to find a studio space and all the other things required to develop his own collections from 2011.

18 A similar, if more elegant and carefully curated, style can be found inside the atelier shops in the Mitte neighbourhood, where older and wealthier tourists and cultural visitors stroll.

19 On several occasions, the designers did a short walkabout with us, describing changes in the neighbourhood in recent years, discussing local politics and offering insights about their wider involvement in the multicultural streets in which they lived and worked and brought up their children.

20 Thanks to Berlin fashion academic Oliver MacConnell, who also acted as a consultant to the CREATe project. Personal communication.

21 Majaco is (or was: as the website for 2021 indicates, the shop is now 'permanently closed') a good example. Over a period of seven years, starting from 2014, they underwent various changes, starting with a well-positioned shop and studio with two young women at the helm. A couple of years later it became a one-woman outfit, and the owner described how she had also decided to reduce the scale and the scope of the collections, having initially attracted a lot of media and good publicity in the city. She had stopped doing shows to cut costs and instead concentrated on basic classics. On one of our visits to the

shop/atelier, we were able to see this in action, with one of the rails full of the same dress in different shades of jersey and in different sizes. On the other rail were tops/blouses, again in the same fabric and colour range. There was space in the shop to do the sampling and pattern cutting and this could also be done when the shop itself was quiet. The designer reported that she had a stable clientele of local people, tourists and visitors to the city. The menswear designer Stefan Dietzelt (Director's Cut) confirmed this picture. He said he had an 'excellent renting situation' for his shop and studio, which he had held onto over the years. He too had been a rising star, attracting large amounts of press and publicity, but more recently he had settled down into a more niche role with a fine range of menswear (jackets, shirts and trousers) with imaginative historic detail in the tailoring and an interesting subcultural edge across the range. This was his repertoire, which he reworked from one year to the next. The busy and trendy location of his shop brought in a regular flow of customers and browsers, an international crowd as well as locals and clubbers. He mentioned that production was also manageable since he was able to use small factories in nearby Poland, just an hour's drive away by car.

22 The Künstlersozialkasse provides cheaper health insurance for cultural workers.

23 And at a later stage, the fact that higher education for young people is also free means that parents do not feel obligated to offer them additional financial support at university, since they will not be burdened by a loans system, as is the case in the UK. A further advantage allows young people to study for a Master's in Germany, which is also free. If they decide to study in the UK, their parents can often help with the fees as they have not had to cover any educational or living costs up to that stage.

24 See Kennel (2022).

25 See https://sqetch.co/creative-city-berlin-interviews-marte-hentschel

26 Carstensen's most recent website mentions that the stones, pearls and crystals come from the Swarovski brand and some references to H&M can also be seen, suggesting that the collaborations sought have recently come to fruition. Also of note on the website is reference to a letter from Michelle Obama congratulating the venture for its valuable work for women's empowerment.

27 A not-for-profit Association for Integration, Education and Arts.

28 Many of the pieces conjure up bridal images or the romance of the boudoir, or they are suggestive of romance and friendship. 'THERESA is a delicate friendship bracelet with Swarovski pearls and crystals. With this purchase you support the empowerment and employment of migrant women from Turkey, Kurdistan, Syria, Lebanon, Pakistan and Kosovo in Berlin. The social commitment of RITA IN PALMA for the women who produce the jewellery on site in Berlin led to the foundation of the non-profit association Von Meisterhand eV. Thank you!' https://www.rita-in-palma.com/products/theresa?variant= 17910787407962.

29 In May 2016, Perbandt gave a talk about her work for the CREATe project at Glasgow School of Art; in January 2017, at the Berlin Fashion Week, she invited the CREATe team to join her as in conversation at Soho House (see Figures 4 and 5).

30 Shop activity, July 2018. Notes from Hannah Curran-Troop: 'From my shop visit, I found that there were two interns working full-time. They appeared to be the only staff. One intern explained that she was doing everything in terms of tasks and responsibilities for Esther's label. She appeared to be not only managing the shop but making samples and cut-outs in the studio in the back room, as well as managing other administrative tasks that Esther needed help with. Her internship was for five months in total. She had studied fashion prior to the internship, and reached out to Esther showing her interest. She was later offered a full-time internship with the label. The other intern I met there was a lot younger, still at university and explained that he was just doing an internship for six weeks in his summer break from studies.'

31 Fashion studies in Germany exists as an off-shoot of art history, and although it is possible to encounter occasional studies of fashion items, for example the skinny jean, in journals such as *Texte zur Kunste*, creative economy approaches to fashion are few and far between (Exner 2011).

Chapter 4: Milan: Fashion Microenterprises and Female-led Artisanship

1 According to www.statista.com, in 2005 14% of graduates in Italy were unemployed, rising to 18% in 2015 and dropping to 10.9% in 2020. However, news reports suggested that

these figures do not take into account informal family-related economic activity.

2 Fab labs were experimental occupied spaces for learning skills with fashion and textiles, plus software programs with a view to creating alternative environmentally friendly fashion.

3 Zoe Romano, Gianino Malossi and Adam Arvidsson

4 If technology has the ability to both free up some time for the workers and also relies on higher levels of cognitive input and sharing of ideas, then the outcome can lead to a more organized and more politicized workforce – i.e., the General Intellect.

5 Instituto Marangoni, originally a tailoring school, opened in 1935. It now runs degree courses accredited both in Italy and for the London school by Manchester Metropolitan University. Its website says that 'students will engage with "Made in Italy" culture and the latest fashion trends'. Domus Academy Milan, opened in 1982, was owned by a publishing family but is not accredited for degree award activity in Italy; like Marangoni, it is now owned by a private equity education company.

6 Camera Nazionale della Moda was founded in 1958 as a nonprofit trade body for Italian fashion based in Milan; and only in recent years were women first voted onto the board.

7 The journal *Conference of Socialist Economics* (CSE) published a range of relevant articles on post-Fordism.

8 See the Introduction, note 3.

9 The volume featured three articles by Geoff Mulgan and two by Charlie Leadbeater, both of whom went on to become close advisers to Tony Blair when he became prime minister.

10 A slogan that was first used in 1980 and was ramped up to encourage export industries from 2014.

11 The CREATe team found itself involved in two such programmes, one in Palermo (2013–14), the other titled Area Progetti in the Venice region (2015–16). Both involved lead partners from outside Italy.

12 'Designers produce innovations. They shape lifestyles. They design the shops which are described as "stages" for the act of shopping … People working in design consultancies are the engineers of designer capitalism' (Murray 1989a: 44).

13 From Fiorucci to Benetton to Vivienne Westwood in Milan.

14 The company then expanded into cottons for denim jeans, shorts, shirts, trousers, etc.

15 This was a time when the ideas of (Gramsci-influenced) Eurocommunism were introduced from Italy to the UK, and these promised a more engaged and dynamic left-wing political economy by tapping into popular culture, including those forms

enjoyed by ordinary working-class people in areas such as fashion and pop music.

16 Laura Bovone (2005) interviewed cultural entrepreneurs in the trendy Ticinese area, commenting on the lively atmosphere and the producers being either old-style 'recycled former artisans' or 'brilliant aesthetes belonging to the latest generation of middle-class professionals who had gentrified the quarter'.

17 This is borne out by a study by D'Ovidio (2019) that included interviews with twenty-six 'early career' and independent fashion designers in and around the city of Milan. She was investigating the networks that this kind of cohort had to navigate in order to get their work seen and recognized. Of the respondents, just over half were able to make a living supplementing their fashion work with support from 'partners, parents or other jobs'.

18 For example, both the Fendi label and Missoni have, in recent decades, given leading roles to women family members – as, of course, has Donatella Versace.

19 The children of prominent fashion dynasties in Italy will often travel to London or New York for their studies, or else they learn the trade within the confines of the family business.

20 On 5 October 2021, Fondazione Santagata Rome announced: 'The start of the second edition of the Fondazione Santagata AWARD is approaching, which will be held as part of the Rome Museum Exhibition and is aimed at international and Italian sustainable development projects ... Projects have to be realized in one of the following sites or communities with UNESCO designation ... World Heritage, Intangible Cultural heritage, Creative Cities, Biosphere Reserves Global Geoparks.' See https://www.fondazionesantagata.it/.

Chapter 5: Click and Collect: Fashion's New Political Economy

1 Reports mention that Zalando has made little clear profit due to its need for constant reinvestment. This has included massive expansion in delivery services and new distribution centres in Germany, France, Poland and Sweden. Overall, the company delivers more than 3,000 brands to fifteen countries.

2 For example, in France the luxury conglomerate LVMH in 2017 launched its own multibrand site called 24 Sèvres, which was itself a successor to their previous eLuxury.com site, which closed in 2009. This had fizzled out because the luxury labels began to develop their own branded sites for online sales. Four

years later, in 2021, the site no longer existed, having been replaced by something called 24S in 2019.

3 At the time of writing, the small vans have been replaced by customized larger black carriers.

4 Vestiaire provides an authentication service after which seller and buyer negotiate for a final price.

5 Of our respondents, only one, Teija Eilola, sells on Farfetch.

6 https://www.dailymail.co.uk/news/article-9125677/Asos-build -giant-90m-warehouse-UK-recruit-2-000-workers.html.

7 Woods (2020) reports that 125,000 jobs were lost in the UK between January and September 2020.

8 See Sweney (2021).

9 Interviewed by Giannino Malossi, Milan 2019.

10 'Wolf & Badger was founded by brothers Henry and George Graham in 2010 with a small boutique in Notting Hill, expanding two years later to a second location in Mayfair. With a high global demand for independent design, Henry and George replicated the physical retail concept in an online platform, wolfandbadger.com. Since then the two London stores have transformed into a three-level, 12,000 square foot department store in Coal Drops Yard, King's Cross, collaborating with restaurant partner hicce … Wolf & Badger is always seeking talented designers to join our platform. Our innovative "serviced retail" concept provides an opportunity for independent brands to showcase and retail their premium collections direct to consumers, through a dedicated space online and in our Wolf & Badger stores in London or New York.' https://bonabag.com/wolf-badger-magazine/.

11 Can we assume a collaboration with the tech scene in Berlin and these more slick e-commerce systems now visible in Berlin? Monies have been made available recently to facilitate this transition.

12 Personal communication from Oliver MacConnell, Berlin, 7 July 2021.

13 We invited Sophie Slater to give a talk to the undergraduate and joint MA course on urban studies at Goldsmiths, University of London, 2016.

14 'Our new collection is a riot of colour. Made in super soft, sustainably sourced fabric, you can pick-n-mix cuts in different fruit salad hues. Frilly collars, puff sleeves, and pink-on-orange gingham are some of the collection's joy-sparking details, designed to break through the monotony of lockdown. Birdsong began life as a feminist brand making slogan tees, shouting about photoshop and hell-bent on paying women workers a

fair wage. A commitment to ethical and sustainable fashion is still at our core, but today we've grown to create a collection of original wardrobe staples to totally transform your (out)look. Birdsong's Facebook page

15 'Not Just A Label (NJAL) brings together a community of the most exciting independent and contemporary emerging talents from over 150 countries across the globe. The NJAL platform helps designers to gain exposure in the fashion industry at no cost, promoting a designer's creativity and individuality above all else ... Siegel went on to earn his MA in International Business Administration in 2004 at the Vienna University of Economics after which he joined the world of finance, working for Ernst & Young and Merrill Lynch, specializing in the Consumer & Retail sector. It was this experience that Stefan used to start Not Just A Label.' https://www.notjustalabel.com.

16 CREATe provided a feature from the research about decentralizing fashion and its spatial logic to be out of London and the capital cities; see McRobbie (2016).

17 'Personalized, tailor-made and delivered directly from the studios of our designers – by investing in sustainable and ethical fashion your purchases will give creative entrepreneurs equitable access to retail their designs globally.' https://www.notjustalabel.com /about/njal.

18 Potential browsing customers, for example, might be tempted by a simple mid-length halter-neck pleated summer dress in two shades by a Singaporean designer JinLee, made to order at £175 (in June 2021).

19 See https://www.ft.com/content/70cb83bf-69dd-4f31-9f01 -162128ff7e7f.

References

Adelfio, M., Hamiduddin, I. and Meidema, E. (2020) 'London's King's Cross Redevelopment: A Compact, Resource Efficient and "Liveable" Global City Model for an Era of Climate Emergency?', *Urban Research and Practice* 14 (2): 180–200.

Alacovska, A. and Gill, R. (2019) 'De-Westernizing Creative Labour Studies: The Informality of Creative Work from an Ex-Centric Perspective', *International Journal of Cultural Studies* 22 (2), 195–212.

Albanese, M. M., Frondizi, R. and Guga, E. (2014) 'Start Ups in the Cultural and Creative Industries: The Main Criticisms in Italy', Conference paper, University of Rome, Tor Vergata, Italy.

Appadurai, A. (ed.) (1988) *The Social Life of Things: Commodities in Cultural Perspective*, Cambridge University Press, Cambridge.

Armstrong, L. (2016) 'Eva Chen on How Instagram Made Fashion More Friendly', *Telegraph*, 2 March.

Arvidsson, A. and Malossi, G. (2010) 'Customer Co-Production from Social Factory to Brand', in Zwick, D. and Cayla, J. (eds), *Inside Marketing*, Oxford University Press, Oxford, pp. 212–233.

Arvidsson, A. and Peitersen, N. (2013) *The Ethical Economy: Re-Building Value after the Crisis*, Columbia University Press, New York.

Arvidsson, A., Malossi, G. and Romano, Z. (2011) 'Passionate Work: Labour Conditions in Italian Fashion', *Journal for Cultural Research* 14 (3): 259–309.

Ayres, J. (2021) 'Enterprising Fashion: The Political Economy of

Vintage, Second-Hand Clothes and Secondary Markets', Doctoral dissertation, New York University.

Bader, I. and Scharenberg, A. (2010) 'The Sound of Berlin: Subculture and the Global Music Industry', *International Journal of Urban and Regional Studies* 34 (1): 76–91.

Bandinelli, C. (2019) *Social Entrepreneurship and Neoliberalism: Making Money while Doing Good*, Rowman and Littlefield, London.

Banks, M. (2020) 'The Work of Culture and C-19', *European Journal of Cultural Studies* 23 (4): 648–654.

Banks, M. and Oakley, K. (2016) 'The dance goes on forever? Art schools, class and UK higher education', *International Journal of Cultural Policy* 22 (1): 41–57.

Banks, M. and O'Connor, J. (2017) 'Inside the Whale (and How to Get Out of There): Moving on from Two Decades of Creative Industries Research', *European Journal of Cultural Studies* 20 (6): 637–654.

Beck, U. (1986) *Risk Society: Towards a New Modernity* (trans. Mark Ritter), Sage, London.

Beck, U. (2000) *The Brave New World of Work*, Polity, Cambridge.

Beck, U. (2016) 'The Cosmopolitan Condition: Why Methodological Nationalism Fails', *Theory, Culture and Society* 24 (7–8): 286–291.

Belfiore, E. (2004) 'The Methodological Challenge of Cross-National Research: Comparing Cultural Policy in Britain and Italy'. Working Paper. Coventry: Centre for Cultural Policy Studies, University of Warwick. Centre for Cultural Policy Studies University of Warwick Research Papers (No. 8).

Benjamin, W. (1979) *Berlin Chronicle 1932*, NLB Books, London.

Bennett, T. (1992) 'Useful Culture', *Cultural Studies*, 6: 395–408.

Bennett, T. (1995) *The Birth of the Museum: History, Theory, Politics*, Routledge, London.

Berardi, F. (2009) *The Soul at Work: From Alienation to Autonomy*, MIT Press, Boston.

Berfelde, R. (forthcoming) 'Airbnb: Leveraging the Crisis of Care to Become Essential Infrastructure', in Into the Black Box (ed.), *On Platforming: Digital Capitalism and Its Aftermath*, University of Bologna Press, Italy.

Berlin Partner GmbH (2005) *Report on Fashion and the Creative Industries*.

Bernt, M. and Holm, A. (2009) 'Is It or Is It Not? The Conceptualisation of Gentrification and Displacement and Its Political Implications in the Case of Berlin-Prenzlauerberg', *City* 13 (2–3): 312–324.

Berry, J. (2015) 'Everyone Is Not an Artist: Autonomous Art Meets the Neoliberal City', *New Formations* 84/85: 20–40.

Bertacchini, E. and Borrione, P. (2010) 'The Geography of the Italian Creative Economy: The Special Role of Design and Craft Industries', *Regional Studies* 47 (2): 135–147.

Bonacich, E. and Appelbaum, R.P. (2000) *Behind the Label: Inequality in the Los Angeles Apparel Industry*, University of California Press, Berkeley.

Born, G. (1995) *Rationalizing Culture: IRCAM, Boulez, and the Institutionalization of the Musical Avant-Garde*, Oxford University Press, Oxford.

Born, G. (2010) 'The Social and the Aesthetic: For a Post-Bourdieuian Theory of Cultural Production', *Cultural Sociology* 4 (2): 171–208.

Born, G. (2013) *Uncertain Vision: Birt, Dyke and the Reinvention of the BBC*, Vintage, London.

Bourriaud, N. (1998) *Relational Aesthetics*, Les Presse du Réele, Paris.

Bovone, L. (2005) 'Fashionable Quarters in the Postindustrial City: The Ticinese of Milan', *City and Community* 4 (4): 359–380.

Bovone, L. (2006) 'Urban Style Culture and Urban Cultural Production in Milan: Postmodern Identity and the Transformation of Fashion', *Poetics* 34 (6): 370–382.

Breward, C. and Gilbert, D. (2006) *Fashion's World Cities*, Berg, Oxford.

British Council Report (2020) *Cultural Value*, London.

Brown, M. and Jones, R. (2021) *Paint Your Town Red: How Preston Took Back Control and Your Town Can Too*, Penguin, London.

Brown, W. (2015) *Undoing the Demos: Neoliberalism's Stealth Revolution*, Princeton University Press, Princeton.

Bull, A. (2019) *Class, Control and Classical Music*, Oxford University Press, Oxford.

Bull, A. and Scharff, C. (2017) '"McDonald's Music" versus "Serious Music": How Production and Consumption Practices Help to Reproduce Class Inequality in the Classical Music Profession', *Cultural Sociology* 11 (3): 283–301.

Business of Fashion (2020) *Annual Fashion Report*, McKinsey and Co., London.

Care Collective, The (2020) *The Care Manifesto*, Verso, London.

Casadei, P., Gilbert, D. and Lazzeretti, L. (2020) 'Urban Fashion Formations in the Twenty-First Century: Weberian Ideal Types as a Heuristic Device to Unravel the Fashion City', *International Journal of Urban and Regional Research* 45 (5): 879–896.

Colomb, C. (2012) 'Pushing the Urban Frontier: Temporary Uses of Space, City Marketing, and the Creative City Discourses in 2000's Berlin', *Journal of Urban Affairs* 34 (2): 131–152.

Cossu, A. (2022) *Autonomous Art Institutions: Artists Disrupting the Creative City*, Rowan and Littlefield, London.

Cox, H. (2022) 'The Global Rental Squeeze', *Financial Times*, 27 April.

Curran, J. and Hesmondhalgh, D. (2019) *Media and Society*, 6th ed. Bloomsbury Academic, London.

D'Ovidio, M. (2019) 'The City as Creative Hub: The Case of the Fashion Industry in Italy', in Gill, R., Pratt, A. C. and Virani, T. E., *Creative Hubs in Question*, Palgrave Macmillan, Basingstoke, pp. 281–298.

D'Ovidio, M. and Cossu, A. (2017) 'Culture is Reclaiming the Creative City: The Case of Macao in Milan', *City, Culture and Society* 8: 7–12.

D'Ovidio, M. and Pradel, M. (2013) 'Social Innovation and Institutionalisation in the Cognitive Cultural Economy: Two Contrasting Experiences from Southern Europe', *Cities* 33: 69–76.

Dowling, E. (2020) *The Crisis in Care*, Verso, London.

Duffy, B. E. (2016) *(Not) Getting Paid To Do What You Love: Gender, Social Media and Aspirational Work*, Yale University Press, New Haven.

du Gay, P. (1997) *Production of Culture/Cultures of Production*, Sage, London.

du Gay, P. and Hall, S. (1997) *Doing Cultural Studies: The Story of the Sony Walkman*, Sage, London.

Dullroy, J. (2020) 'The Politics of the Rent Cap', *Exberliner*, 20 August. https://www.exberliner.com/politics/politics-under-the -cap/.

Dunford, M. (2006) 'Industrial Districts, Magic Circles and the Restructuring of the Italian Textiles and Clothing Chain', *Economic Geography* 82 (1): 27–59.

Elan, P. (2016) 'Why Money More Than Talent is Now Key to Fashion Education', *Guardian*, 6 June.

Entwistle, J. and Slater, D. (2014) 'Reassembling the Cultural: Fashion Models, Brands and the Meaning of "Culture" after ANT', *Journal of Cultural Economy* 7 (2): 161–177.

Exner, M. (2011) 'Fashion and the City: How the Built Environment Mediates Berlin's Rise as a Fashion Capital', Master's thesis, London School of Economics.

Fantone, L. (2007) 'Precarious Changes: Gender and Generational Politics in Contemporary Italy', *Feminist Review* 87: 5–20.

Fashion Roundtable (2021) *Follow Up Report, Brexit: The Impact on the Fashion Industry*, London.

Fernie, J. and Grant, N. (2019) *Fashion Logistics*, Routledge, London.

Florida, R. (2004) *The Rise of the Creative Class*, Basic Books, New York.

Florida, R. (2017) *The New Urban Crisis: How Our Cities Are Increasing Inequality, Deepening Segregation and Failing the Middle Classes*, Hachette, New York.

Fostering Sustainable Practices (FSP) (2021) University of the Arts, London. www/sustainable-fashion-com/ fostering-sustainable-practices.

Foucault, M. (1991) *Selected Writing*, Penguin, London.

Foucault, M. (2004) *Society Must Be Defended*, Penguin, London.

Frith, S. (1981) *Sound Effects: Youth, Leisure and the Politics of Rock 'n' Roll*, Routledge, London.

Frith, S. and Horne, H. (1987) *Art into Pop*, Methuen, London.

Fuller, M. and Weizman, E. (2021) *Investigative Aesthetics: Conflicts and Commons in the Politics of Truth*, Verso, London.

Giddens, A. (1998) *The Third Way*, Polity, Cambridge.

Gross, J. (2020) *The Birth of the Creative Industries Revisited: An Oral History of the 1998 DCMS Mapping Document.* King's College London. https://kclpure.kcl.ac.uk/portal/files/125010567 /Gross_J._2020_The_Birth_of_the_Creative_Industries_Revisited .pdf.

Hadjimichalis, C. (2006) 'The End of the Third Italy As We Knew It?' *Antipode* 38 (1): 82–106.

Hall, S. (1988) *The Hard Road to Renewal: Thatcherism and the Crisis of the Left*, Verso, London.

Hall, S. and Jacques, M. (1989) *New Times: The Changing Face of Politics in the 1990s*, Lawrence and Wishart, London.

Hall, Z. D. (2021) 'In Berlin 85% of People Rent Their Homes and Prices Are Spiralling', *Financial Times*, 22 October.

Hardt, D. and Negri, T. (2000) *Empire,* Harvard University Press, Boston.

Harris, J., Begum, L. and Vecchi, A. (2021) *Business of Fashion, Textiles & Technology: Summary Report: Mapping the UK Fashion, Textiles and Technology Ecosystem*, University of the Arts, London.

Harvey, D. (2001) *Spaces of Capital: Towards a Critical Geography*, Routledge, London.

Harvey, D. (2002) 'The Art of Rent: Globalization Monopoly and the Commodification of Culture', *Socialist Register* 34: 93–110.

Harvey, D. (2008) 'The "New" Imperialism: Accumulation by Dispossession', *Socialist Register* 64: 63–87.

Harvey, D. (2012) *Rebel Cities*, Verso, London.

Hebdige, R. (1978) *Subculture: The Meaning of Style*, Methuen, London.

Hesmondhalgh, D. (1997) 'Post-Punk's Attempts to Democratise the Music Industry: The Success and Failure of Rough Trade', *Popular Music* 16 (3): 255–274.

Hesmondhalgh, D. (1999) 'Indie: The Institutional Politics and Aesthetics of a Popular Music Genre', *Cultural Studies* 13 (1): 34–61.

Hesmondhalgh, D., Oakley, K., Lee, D. and Nisbett, M. (2018) *Culture, Economy, Politics: The Case of New Labour*, Palgrave, London.

Hitchen, G. and Vaz, F. (2021) 'Creative Innovation in Times of Covid'. https://craic.lboro.ac.uk/essays/creative-innovation-in-the-time-of-covid/.

Hoskins, T. E. (2014) *Stitched Up: The Anti-Capitalist Book of Fashion*, Counterfire, London.

Jakob, D. (2009) *Beyond Creative Production Networks: The Development of Intra Metropolitan Creative Industry Clusters in Berlin and New York*, Rhombos, Berlin.

Kalandides, A. (2014) *Report on Berlin Fashion Micro-Producers*, CREATe, AHRC, University of Glasgow.

Kennel, P. (2022) (forthcoming) 'Social Entrepreneurship Discourse(s) in Germany: The First Two Decades', PhD thesis, Goldsmiths, University of London.

Kneese, T. and Palm, M. (2020) 'Brick-and-Platform: Listing Labour in the Digital Vintage Economy', *Social Media + Society*, July–September. https://journals.sagepub.com/doi/10.1177/2056305120933299.

Kozlowski, M. et al. (eds) (2013) *Joy Forever: The Political Economy of Social Creativity*, MayFly Books, Poland.

Lange, B. (2012) 'Value Creation in the Creative Economy: The Case of Electronic Club Music in Germany', *Economic Geography* 82 (2): 149–169.

Lange, B. (2016) 'Labs: Places of Hope', *Creative City Magazine*, Berlin.

Lash, S. and Urry, J. (1994) *The Economy of Signs and Spaces*, Sage, London.

Lazzarato, M. (1996) 'Immaterial Labour', in Virno, P. and Hardt, M. (eds), *Radical Thought in Italy: A Potential Politics*, University of Minnesota Press, Minneapolis, pp. 133–147.

Lindberg, M., Forsberg, L. and Karlberg, H. (2015) 'Gendered

References	177

Social Innovation: A Theoretical Lens for Analysing Structural Transformations in Organisations and Society', *International Journal of Social Entrepreneurship and Innovation* 3 (6): 472–483.
Loewe, M. (2013) 'The City as Experiential Space: The Production of Meaning', *International Journal of Urban and Regional Research* 37 (3): 894–909.
Lorey, I. (2015) *State of Insecurity: Government of the Precarious*, Verso, London.
Malossi, G. (2002) *Designing Value: The First Survey of Intellectual Properties in the Fields of Industrial Design and Fashion*, Report for Meers Pierson, Italy.
Manske, A. (2021) 'Torn Between the Old and the New World of Work: Insights into the Modernised Semi-Profession of the Fashion Industry', *Management Revue* 32 (3): 244–265.
Marx, K. (1993) *Grundrisse*, Penguin, London.
Max, D. T. (2018) 'The Chinese Workers Who Assemble Designer Bags in Tuscany', *The New Yorker*, 29 March.
McGarvey, D. (2017) *Poverty Safari*, Luath Press, Edinburgh.
McGettigan A (2013) *The Great University Gamble: Money, Markets and the Future of Education*, Pluto Press, London.
McGuigan, J. (2005) 'Neoliberalism, Culture and Policy', *International Journal of Cultural Policy* 11 (3): 229–241.
McRobbie, A. (1994) 'Second-Hand Dresses and the Role of the Ragmarket', in *Postmodernism and Popular Culture*, Routledge, London, pp. 135–154.
McRobbie, A. (1998) *British Fashion Design: Rag Trade or Image Industry?* Routledge, London.
McRobbie, A. (2016) *Be Creative: Making a Living in the New Culture Industries*, Polity, Cambridge.
McRobbie, A., Strutt, D. and Bandinelli, C. (2016) *Fashion Micro-Enterprises in London, Berlin and Milan*, Project Report, CREATe, Glasgow University and Goldsmiths, University of London.
Mead, R. (2010) 'The Prince of Solomeo: The Cashmere Utopia of Brunello Cucinello', *The New Yorker*, 29 March.
Mensitieri, G. (2021) *The Most Beautiful Job in the World*, Bloomsbury Academic, London.
Mezzadri, A. (2017) *The Sweatshop Regime: Labouring Bodies, Exploitation and Garments 'Made in India'*, Cambridge University Press, Cambridge.
Minton, A. (2017) *Big Capital: Who Is London For?* Penguin, London.
Mole, N. J. (2010) 'Precarious Subjects: Anticipating Neoliberalism in Northern Italy's Workplace', *American Anthropologist* 112 (12): 38–53.

Molotch, H. (2003) *Where Stuff Comes From: How Toasters, Toilets, Cars and Computers Come to Be the Way They Are*, Routledge, New York.

Montalto, V. (2010) 'Decentralisation and Devolution in Italian Cultural Politics: How Micro Practices Should Inspire Macro Policies', *Cultural Trends* 19 (1–2): 15–25.

Moore, R. (2016) *Slow Burn City: London in the 21st Century*, Picador, London.

Moore, S. (2015) 'Our Art Schools Have Become Finishing Schools for the Wealthy Few', *Guardian*, 15 April.

Mora, E. (2006) 'Collective Production of Creativity in the Italian Fashion System', *Poetics* 34 (6): 334–353.

Moreno, L. (2014) 'The Urban Process under Financialised Capitalism', *City* 18 (3): 244–268.

Moreno, L. (2018a) 'Always Crashing in the Same City: Real Estate, Psychic Capital and Planetary Desire', *City* 22 (1): 152–168.

Moreno, L. (2018b) 'The Urban Regeneration of the Plantation Age', unpublished paper, Goldsmiths, University of London.

Moules, J. (2021) 'Keeping Staff and Clients on Board in a Pandemic', *Financial Times*, 26 July.

Murray, R. (1989a) 'Benetton Britain', in Hall, S. and Jacques, M. (eds), *New Times: The Changing Face of Politics in the 1990s*, Lawrence and Wishart, London.

Murray, R. (1989b) 'Fordism and Post-Fordism', in Hall, S. and Jacques, M. (eds), *New Times: The Changing Face of Politics in the 1990s*, Lawrence and Wishart, London.

Nixon, S. (1996) *Hard Looks: Masculinities, Spectatorship and Contemporary Consumption*, Palgrave, Basingstoke.

Oakley, K. and O'Brien, D. (2016) 'Learning to Labour Unequally: Understanding the Relationship between Cultural Production, Cultural Consumption and Inequality', *Social Identities* 22 (5): 471–486.

Oakley, K. and Ward, J. (2018) 'Creative Economy, Critical Perspectives', *Cultural Trends* 27 (5): 311–312.

O'Brien, D. (2008) *Measuring the Value of Culture*, DCMS, London.

O'Brien, D., Allen, K., Friedman, S. and Saha, A. (2017) 'Producing and Consuming Inequality: A Cultural Sociology of the Culture Industries', *Cultural Sociology* 11 (3): 271–282.

O'Brien, D., Brook, O. and Taylor, M. (2018) 'Panic: Social Class, Taste and Inequalities in the Creative Industries'. www .createlondon.org/event/panic-paper.

O'Brien, D., Friedman, S. and McDonald, I. (2021) 'Deflecting

Privilege: Class, Identity and the Intergenerational Self', *Sociology* 55 (4): 716–733.

Osborne, H. (2014) 'Poor Doors: The Segregation of London's Inner-City Flat Dwellers', *Guardian*, 25 July.

Oxford Economics (2021) 'The Status of German Fashion', Fashion Council Germany. https://www.oxfordeconomics.com/resource /the-status-of-german-fashion/.

Peck, J. (2005) 'Struggling with the Creative Class', *International Journal of Urban and Regional Studies* 29 (4): 740–770.

Peter, E. (2021) 'Next Level of the Berlin Rent Cap: Bad Image Big Impact', *Taz Berlin*, 2 March. https://taz.de/naechste-stufe-des -Berliner-Mietendeckels/!5725820/.

Pisoni, A. (2012) 'Start-Ups in Italy: Facts and Trends', Mind the Bridge Survey 2012, CrESIT, Varese.

Pollert, A. (1988) 'Dismantling Flexibility', *Capital and Class* 12 (1): 42–75.

Rancière, J. (2008) *The Emancipated Spectator*, Verso, London.

Raunig, G. (2013) *Factories of Knowledge: Industries of Creativity*, Semiotext(e), Cambridge, MA.

Rocamora, A. (2011) 'Personal Fashion Blogs: Screens and Mirrors in Digital Self-Portraits', *Fashion Theory* 15 (4): 407–424.

Rocamora, A. (2017) 'Mediatization and Digital Media in the Field of Fashion', *Fashion Theory* 21 (5): 505–522.

Rocamora, A. (2022) 'Mediatization and Digital Retail', in Geczy, A. and Karaminas, V. (eds), *The End of Fashion: Clothing and Dress in the Age of Globalisation*, Bloomsbury, London.

Romano, Z. (2018) 'Fablab e Makerspace: Co-costruire l'innovazione fuori dall'accademia', *Scienziati in affanno?*, CNR, May.

Ross, A. (ed.) (2000) *No Sweat: Fashion, Free Trade, and the Rights of Garment Workers*, Verso, New York.

Ross, A. (2004) 'Made in Italy: The Trouble with Craft Capitalism', *Antipode* 36 (2): 209–216.

Ross, A. (2013) *Creditocracy and the Case for Debt Refusal*, OR Books, New York.

Rossiter, N. (2014) 'Logistical Worlds', *Cultural Studies Review* 20 (1): 53–76.

Rullani E. (1997) 'L'evoluzione dei distretti industriali: Un percorso tra decostruzione e internazionalizzazione', in Varaldo R. and Ferrucci L. (eds), *Il distretto industriale tra logiche di impresa e logiche di Sistema*, F. Angeli, Milano.

Saha, A. (2019) *Race and the Culture Industries*, Sage, London.

Sandoval, M. and Littler, J. (2019) 'Creative Hubs: A Co-operative Space', in Gill, R., Pratt, A. C. and Virani, T. E. (eds),

Creative Hubs in Question, Palgrave Macmillan, Basingstoke, pp. 155–168.

Sassen, S. (1991) *The Global City: New York, London and Tokyo*, Princeton University Press, Princeton.

Sassen, S. (2002) 'Transnationalization of Labour', in Bridge, G. and Watson, S. (eds), *The Blackwell City Reader*, Blackwell, Oxford.

Scharff, C. (2017) *Gender, Subjectivity and Cultural Work: The Classical Music Profession*, Routledge, London.

Schlesinger, P. (2013) 'Expertise, the Academy and the Governance of Cultural Policy', *Media Culture and Society* 35 (1): 27–35.

Schwanhaeuser, A. (2010) *Kosmonauten der Berliner Underground: Ethnografie einer Berliner Szene*, Campus Verlag GmbH, Frankfurt.

Scott, A. J. (2000) *The Cultural Economy of Cities: Essays on the Geography of Image-Producing Industries*, Sage, New York.

Simmel, G. (1957[1904]) 'Fashion', *American Journal of Sociology* 62 (6): 541–558.

Standing, G. (2015) *The Precariat: The New Dangerous Class*, Bloomsbury, London.

Steele, V. (2003) *Fashion, Italian Style*, Yale University Press, New Haven.

Stevens, Q. and Ambler, M. (2010) 'Europe's City Beaches as Post-Fordist Place-Making', *Journal of Urban Design* 15: 515–537.

Sullivan, A. (2021) 'Berliners Vote "Yes" on Property Expropriation, But What Happens Now?' *Deutsche Welle*, 27 September. https://www.dw.com/en/berliners-vote-yes-on-property-expropriation-but-what-happens-now/a-59070328.

Sullivan, A. (2022) 'Britain's "Dark Factories": Specters of Racial Capitalism Today', *Fashion Theory* 26 (4): 493–508.

Sweney, M. (2021) 'Amazon Creates 10,000 UK Jobs on the Back of Online Shopping Boom', *Guardian*, 14 May.

Tapper, J. (2021) 'Beat That: Berlin's Techno DJs Seek UNESCO World Heritage Status', *Guardian*, 5 December.

Terranova, T. (2004) *Free Labour*, Pluto Press, London.

Thornton, S. (1996) *Club Cultures*, Polity, Cambridge.

Trautvetter, S. (2020) 'Who Owns Berlin?', *Exberliner*. https://www.exberliner.com/politics/who-owns-berlin/.

Ugelvig, J. (2020) *Fashion Work 1993–2018: 25 Years of Art in Fashion*, Damiani, Italy.

Unioncamere/Symbola (2013) 'Italian Quality and Beauty: Compact Report on Cultural and Creative Industries in Italy', *I Quaderni di Symbola*. https://kipdf.com/download/italian-quality-and-beauty-compact-report-on-the-cultural-and-creative-industrie_5aefb7a97f8b9a44268b4587.html.

Vanni, I. (2016) 'Why Save the World When You Can Design It? Precarity and Fashion in Italy', *Fashion Theory* 16 (4): 441–460.

Virno, P. and Hardt, D. (1996) *Radical Thought in Italy: A Potential Politics*, University of Minnesota Press, Minneapolis.

Vishmidt, M. (2009) 'Situation Wanted: Something About Labour', *Afterall Journal* 19: 20–34.

Vishmidt, M. (2019) *Speculation as a Mode of Production*, Brill Books, Berlin.

Volonte, P. (2012) 'Social and Cultural Features of Fashion Design in Milan', *Fashion Theory* 16 (4): 399–431.

von Osten, M. and Barnes, C. (2015) http://www.on-curating .org/issue-19-reader/marion-von-osten-on-her-collaborative-style -and-multiple-roles.html#.Wka1EN9l82w.

Wainwright, O. (2022) '"A Massive Betrayal": How London's Olympic Legacy Was Sold Out', *Guardian*, 29 June.

Westphal, U. (2020) *Fashion Metropolis Berlin: The Story of the Rise and Destruction of the Jewish Fashion Industry* (trans. Kristine Jennings), Henschel Verlag, Berlin.

Wilson, E. (1983) *Adorned in Dreams*, Virago, London.

Wissinger, E. (2015) '#NoFilter: Models, Glamour Labor and the Age of the Blink', *Interface* 1 (1): 1–20.

Wollen, P. (2003) 'The Concept of Fashion in The Arcades Project', *boundary 2: An International Journal of Literature and Culture* 30 (1): 131–142.

Woods, Z. (2020) 'Online Shopping Makes Many High Street Jobs Unviable, Says NEXT Boss', *Guardian*, 25 September.

Wowereit, K., Junge-Reyer, I., Wolf, H. and Walther, I. (2008) *Creative Industries in Berlin: Development and Potential*, Senate Department for Economics, Technology and Women's Issues, Berlin.

Zukin, S. (1989) *Loft Living: Culture and Capital in Urban Change*, Rutgers University Press, New York.

Further Reading

Abboud, L. (2021) 'LVMH Settles Claim that Ex-Intelligence Boss Spied on Maker of Arnault Film', *Financial Times*, 18 December.

Ahlfeldt, G. (2010) 'Blessing or Curse? Appreciation Amenities and Resistance around Berlin Mediaspree', *Hamburg Contemporary Economic Discussions*, 32.

Banks, M. (2017) *Creative Justice: Cultural Industries, Work and Inequality*, Rowman and Littlefield, London.

Banks, M. and O'Connor, J. (2009) 'After the Creative Industries', *International Journal of Cultural Policy* 15 (4): 365–373.

Born, G. and Barry, A. (2018) 'Music Mediation Theories and Actor Network Theory', *Contemporary Music Review* 37 (5–6): 443–487.

Breward, C. (2016) *The Suit: Function, Form, Style*, Reaktion Books, London.

Capone, F. and Lazaretti, L. (2016) 'Fashion and City Branding: An Analysis of the Perception of Florence as a Fashion City', *Journal of Global Fashion Marketing* 7 (3): 160–180.

Economist, The (2021) 'Shein', 9 October.

Fashion Roundtable (2018) 'Brexit and the Impact on the Fashion Industry', London, 29 March. https://www.fashionroundtable.co.uk/news/2018/4/1/fashion-roundtable-brexit-and-the-impact-on-the-fashion-industry-paper.

Gill, R. (2009) 'Breaking the Silence: The Hidden Injuries of Neoliberal Academia', in Flood, R. and Gill, R. (eds), *Secrecy and Silence in the Research Process: Feminist Reflections*, Routledge, London, pp. 228–244.

Gill, R. and Pratt, A. (2009) 'In the Social Factory', *Theory, Culture and Society* 25 (7–8): 1–30.

Hesmondhalgh, D. (2006) *The Cultural Industries*, 4th ed. Sage, London.

Hussein, D. (2021) 'ASOS Will Build Giant £90m Warehouse in the UK and Recruit 2,000 Workers in the Next 3 Years', *Daily Mail*, 8 January.

Lazzarato, M. (2012) *The Making of Indebted Man*. Semiotext(e), Cambridge, MA.

Nguyen, T. (2021) 'Shein is the Future of Fast Fashion. Is It Ethical?' https://www.vox.com/the-goods/22573682/shein-future -of-fast-fashion-explained.

Oakley, K. (2018) 'Good Work? Rethinking Cultural Entrepreneurship', in Bilton, C. and Cummings, S. (eds), *Handbook of Management and Creativity*. Edward Elgar, Cheltenham, pp. 145–159.

Oakley, K., Laurison, D., O'Brien, D. and Friedman, S. (2017) 'Cultural Capital: Arts Graduates, Spatial Inequality, and London's Impact on Cultural Labor Markets', *American Behavioral Scientist* 61 (12): 1510–1531.

O'Connor, J. (1996) 'A Close Look at Regeneration and Business', *City* 1: 167–170.

O'Connor, J. (2021) 'The Great Deflation: Arts and Culture After the Creative Industries', *Making and Breaking*, 02. https:// makingandbreaking.org/article/the-great-deflation-arts-and -culture-after-the-creative-industries/.

O'Connor, J. and Wynne, D. (1997) 'From the Margins to the Centre: Post-Industrial City Cultures', in Sulkunen, P., Holmwood, J., Rader, H. and Schulze, G. (eds), *Constructing the New Consumer*, Palgrave, Basingstoke, pp. 152–172.

Royal Society for the Arts (2021) 'Fast Fashion's Plastic Problem', Policy Briefing, June. https://www.thersa.org/reports/fast-fashions -plastic-problem.

Rowland, S. (2020) Paper presented at Innovative Methodologies in Fashion Studies Research, November, Goldsmiths, University of London.

Saha, A. (2017) 'The Politics of Race in Cultural Distribution: Addressing Inequalities in British Asian Theatre', *Cultural Sociology* 11 (3): 302–317.

Schlesinger, P., Selfe, M. and Munro, E. (2015) *Curators of Cultural Enterprise: A Critical Analysis of a Creative Business Intermediary*, Palgrave Macmillan, Basingstoke.

Senate Berlin (2021) '*Neustarthilfe* Berlin: New Corona Aid for the Self-Employed and Small Businesses', Department of

Economy, Energy and Businesses, Berlin. Press Release. 23 February.

Sinclair, R. (2015) 'Dorcas Legacies, Dorcas Futures: Textile Legacies and the Formation of Identities in "Habitus" Spaces', *Craft Research* 6 (2): 209–222.

Srnicek, N. (2017) *Platform Capitalism*, Wiley, Oxford.

Watt, P. (2013) '"It's Not for Us": Regeneration in the 2012 Olympics and the Gentrification of East London', *City* 17 (1): 99–118.

White, E. (2021) 'Beijing's Top Court Brands Tech Sector Overtime Culture Illegal: The 996 Week of Alibaba', *The Financial Times*, 21 April.

White, N. (2000) *Reconstructing Italian Fashion America and the Development of the Italian Fashion Industry*, Bloomsbury, London.

Wittel, A. (2000) 'Towards a Theory of Network Sociality', *Theory, Culture and Society* 18 (6): 51–76.

Wright, R. and Wilson, P. (2021) 'Crying Shame Behind Boohoo's Leicester's Suppliers', *Financial Times*, 11 July.

Index

Brexit 1, 2, 3, 149–51
  and cultural policy 24
  hurdles to fashion industry
    posed by 28, 60–1,
    149–50
  and the *milieu of labour* 28,
    163n.11
  and UK universities 149
British Fashion Council 26, 50,
    54, 60, 140
Brooke, Chris 31, 38, 64–6,
    135
Brown, Wendy 41
Browns of London 125
The Business of Fashion (online
    journal) 4

Cameron, David 84
Capone, Francesco 110
Carstensen, Ann-Kathrin 86–7,
    136, 165n.26
Castro, Orsola de 140
Central Saint Martins (CSM)
    46, 51, 55, 56, 64, 65,
    76, 92, 122, 142
Centre for Sustainable Fashion
    147
Checinska, Christine 54, 56–7
Chen, Eva 128
China 7, 144
circuit of culture 19
  and art theory 35–6
  and the fashion object 39–40
class 18–19, 25, 26
Clean Clothes Campaign 147
click and collect *see*
    fashion-tech/e-commerce
climate crisis 2, 7, 151
  and fashion-tech 128–9, 133
Clipper 132
club culture fashion
  Berlin 12, 77–8, 90
  London 90
Cockpit, the 161–2n.30

commodity fetishism 7
the commons, and art theory
    33–4, 35
Conran, Terence 107
consumer culture 19, 39, 50–2,
    60, 75, 91, 107, 113
  post-Fordist 105
  upmarket 78
Cornwall 60–1
Cossu, Alberto 98
Covid-19 pandemic 1, 3, 4, 8,
    60, 87, 149, 159n.7
  and e-commerce 126, 133–4,
    135, 136, 144, 145
CREATe research project 41,
    44, 56, 59–60, 61, 68,
    149
  and fashion-tech 134, 136
  and Milan 97, 98, 112
creative economy
  fashion as 5–9, 10
  Italy 99
  United Kingdom 101–3
  urban creative economy in
    Milan 110–11
Creative Industries Federation
    24
creative industry studies 3, 10
critical fashion studies 15–16,
    17–40
  and art theory 20–1, 31–6
  and cultural policy 22–6
  and the fashion object 37–40
  milieu of labour 17, 20–2,
    26–31
CSM *see* Central Saint Martins
Cucinello, Brunello 100
cultural imperialism 20
cultural policy discourse 22–6
  participatory approach to
    23–4
culture, circuit of *see* circuit of
    culture
Curran, James 18

Vestiaire Collective 126, 135
Vinciguerra, Camilla 110,
    112–13, 114, 115
Vinted 133
Virno, Paulo 32
Vishmidt, Marina 34
Vogue magazine
  British 26, 54, 64, 148
  German 89
  Italian 61, 63
Volonte, Paolo 96, 110
Volpi, Carlo 61–4, 134
von Osten, Marion 32–3

wage stagnation
  in Berlin 72, 73
  and Brexit 151
  in the UK 45, 67
Ward, Jonathan 23
Westphal, Uwe 74
Westwood, Vivienne 28, 143
Whistles 53
Williams, Bethany 68, 158n.26
Williams, Dilys 151
Wilson, Harold 20
Wolf & Badger 134, 169n.10
women
  exploitation of 148
  Berlin 12, 69–70, 73, 77,
    85–90, 92

migrant labour 4–5
Milan 13–14, 98–9, 100,
    110–20, 121–2
  working with disadvantaged
    women 151
working-class culture
  and fashion designers 18–19,
    26, 42
working-class people
  academics and wage
    degradation 67–8
  marginalization and
    inequalities 25
  and a 'social fashion' system
    147

YOOX Net-a-Porter 125–6
Young British Designers
    134–5
youth culture
  and the fashion industry
    18–19
  and fashion-tech 127–8

Zalando 15, 123–4, 127, 136,
    168n.1
Zappos.com 124
Zara 126
zero-hours contracts 34, 127,
    159–60n.8